Sunset

GARDEN & PATIO BUILDING BOOK

By the Editors of Sunset Books and Sunset Magazine

Lane Books · Menlo Park, California

How to build it? This book shows you

The editors of Sunset have long recognized the need for a basic book on outdoor building that could be used time and again as a reference by homeowners—whether they be handyman types or all-thumbs suburbanites faced with the necessity of building a fence or constructing a patio overhead. Behind the extensive research and planning for this book was a primary objective: to present in pictorial fashion the best known and recognized building materials and procedures, combined with imaginative new techniques and ideas.

Lending an invaluable hand in the selection of material and the final checking was Tom Riley, Crafts Editor of Sunset Magazine. E. D. Bills, one of the nation's foremost garden illustrators, created the hundreds of drawings that appear throughout the book.

This building guide is intended to take its place as a companion volume to the basic guide for all green-thumbers, *Basic Gardening Illustrated*. It is not to be confused with Sunset's *Garden and Patio Book* of former years, a giant volume that consisted of five complete Sunset building books bound together.

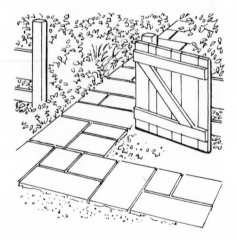

Seventh Printing February 1972

Table of Contents

Special Features

How to set and align fence posts

Sooner or later most homeowners face the prospect of building a fence. Probably the most involved part of this task is setting and aligning the fence posts. The suggestions on these two pages may make your next fence-setting job go more smoothly.

For long fence life, use posts of Western red cedar or California redwood. These woods inhibit the decay-causing action of fungus and insects. Specify *heartwood,* the reddish brown wood from the central part of the tree; sapwood, the lighter wood close to the bark, is much less durable. Mountain cypress, sometimes sold in the Southwest for fence posts, seems to endure as well as cedar and redwood.

DIGGING THE HOLES

For low fences, sink the posts at least 18 inches into the ground. For fences 4 to 6 feet high, sink the posts at least 2 feet; the deeper the better, especially if you want the completed fence to present a solid barrier to winds.

Moisture should be able to drain past the bottom of the posts. For this reason dig holes 4 to 6 inches deeper than the posts will be set, and fill the bottom with rocks and gravel. In clay soil, it's wise to go down even farther, to provide a foot-deep drainage basin of gravel beneath each post.

Locate the fence's corner points, if not self-evident, by using a string and guides called *batter boards* (see diagram). Mark the string every 6 or 8 feet depending on the post spacing you

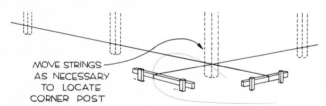

MOVE STRINGS AS NECESSARY TO LOCATE CORNER POST

Batter boards in firm ground near corners to help you position the posts precisely. Mark the string for post spacing desired.

desire. (Although either spacing allows for the most economical use of standard lumber lengths, other spacing may often be dictated by the type of fence, the appearance desired, or the slope of the ground.) Over uneven ground, drop a plumb line from each string mark to pinpoint post locations, and drive in marker stakes. Then begin digging.

Digging tools. Of the two most popular hole-digging tools, the auger type is good to use in rock-free earth, the clamshell type better in rocky soil. In soil that is extremely rocky, a digging bar and a spoon-bladed shovel may be the only combination that will work. Digging is still tough work even with these tools, but the resulting hole (especially with the auger) is much slimmer than with pick and shovel digging, and gives better support for posts and backfill. And less fill is required — an important consideration if you are setting the posts in concrete.

If you have more than six holes to dig, and the earth is not too rocky, power diggers are certainly worth investigation. One-man and two-man power augers are often available at tool rental shops. A rented jackhammer equipped with a spading tip could also do the job. The jackhammer is often the tool of

choice in areas of the Southwest where a hard layer of gravel and rock lies beneath the soil surface.

SETTING POSTS IN EARTH AND GRAVEL FILL

Where the soil is stable (not subject to sliding, cracking, frost heaving), backfilling with earth or earth-and-gravel works fine for most fence posts.

Dump a big base stone into each post hole, or use a few smaller stones, or several inches of gravel. Tamp well, using a good-sized length of 2 by 4 lumber. Set in the post, and shovel in gravel a little at a time while you adjust the post until it's aligned and vertical. Continue filling with earth, earth-and-gravel, or gravel, tamping firmly every 2 or 3 inches. If the hole

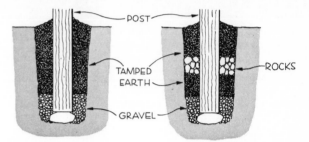

POST — TAMPED EARTH — GRAVEL — ROCKS

Vigorous tamping of the earth is the key to successful use of earth fill. Rocks near the top also help to stabilize the post.

is wide, big rocks jammed around the post near the surface will minimize side movement. Slope the top of the fill so that water will run away from the post. In light, sandy soil — which offers easy shoveling but poor stability for fence posts — nail 1 by 4 cleats of heartwood cedar or redwood across the fence posts near ground level.

SETTING POSTS IN CONCRETE

Concrete fill can use up a surprising amount of cement, sand, and gravel — but it gives the strongest setting by far. The concrete should be angled down at ground line to divert water away from the post. Don't let concrete get *under* the post, where it could hold in moisture and speed decay. Above all, never set fence post ends completely in concrete.

For fence post setting in concrete, you can use a lean mix, with only a third the cement needed for a walkway mix. A mix of 1 part (by volume) cement, 3 parts sand, and 5 parts gravel is good. Keep the mix rather dry. To extend the mix, keep a

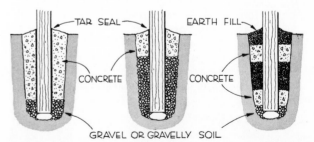

TAR SEAL — EARTH FILL — CONCRETE — CONCRETE — GRAVEL OR GRAVELLY SOIL

Concrete fills using various amounts of concrete. The first two are best for wet climates. Avoid getting concrete under post.

supply of washed rocks on hand, and place them around the perimeter of the holes as you pour.

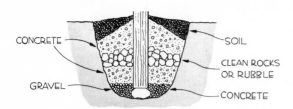

Extending concrete with boulders reduces cost and makes a solid footing in large holes. Add tamped soil on top of the fill.

Using dry concrete mixes (cement, sand, and gravel all in one bag) saves ordering time and trouble, and means you won't have leftover sand or gravel to dispose of. You will need about a bag of mix to pour around a 4-inch post, sunk 2 feet in about a 10-inch diameter hole.

Posts freshly set in concrete can be forced into a new position for perhaps 20 minutes after the pour; they should then be left alone for two days before boards or stringers are nailed on. During a spell of dry weather, fill the small crack between post and concrete with tar or caulking compound.

Frost heaving. Heavy frosts bring two problems: frost heaving, and concrete cracking. To minimize damage from heaving, dig post holes down to a foot below normal frost line; shovel in gravel; drive nails into the sides of each post near its bottom end, and place this end in gravel; pour concrete around nail area; complete the fill by using gravel or gravelly soil.

To prevent concrete collars from cracking when wet posts freeze and expand, cut shingles to width of posts, oil them, and

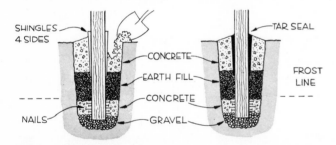

Remove shingles after concrete has set; pour tar between post and concrete to create expansion collar and minimize cracking.

place alongside each post before you pour. When concrete has set, remove the shingles and fill the open spaces with tar or sand.

ALIGNING THE POSTS

Many people consider the aligning of fence posts to be one of the knottiest problems associated with building a fence. Among the many procedures in use, three of the most workable are described below.

Corner post method. This involves setting corner posts first: firmly, permanently, exactly vertical, and with their faces in flat alignment. When they are solidly in place, stretch aligning strings between corner posts, top and bottom. Mark points on

the top line to indicate where the centers of the intermediate posts will be, and transfer the marks, using a plumb bob, to the lower line. Set each intermediate post in gravel, with its face brushing (but not distorting) the aligning strings. Backfill carefully, checking to see that each post remains vertical as you work.

If rough posts snag the aligning strings, slip a piece of ¼-inch material between each corner post and the strings, then nail it on. With batter boards (see method below), move both ends of the cord ¼-inch. Then keep each intermediate post the same ¼-inch distance from the strings. Once all posts

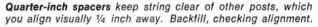

Quarter-inch spacers keep string clear of other posts, which you align visually ¼ inch away. Backfill, checking alignment.

are in, make a final check by eye. (You can correct any misalignment at this time by pushing the post into the correct position and retamping the concrete or earth fill.)

Batter board method. With this method you lay out fence post locations first, then set the posts successively. First, build batter boards (see the sketch on the opposite page) and mark the intended post centers on the aligning string. Continue as in the corner post method—but this time you will have only one string to guide you, and you'll need to check verticals frequently with a level or plumb line.

Here's a tip for plumb line users: Wrap the line around a piece of scrap wood half as thick as the bob is wide. Hold this block against any top corner of the post. When the plumb line lines up with the corner edge, and the bob is brushing the wood, the post is vertical.

One-man method. The "stake-out" method makes it possible for a man working alone to align a fence. Drive two stakes into firm ground near each post, as shown in the sketch below, and nail an arm to each stake. Set posts onto rock or gravel at the bottom of the hole, checking alignment against the string. Use a level or a plumb bob to true one face of the post. Then tack its support arm in place. Do the same for the adjacent face. Check both verticals again, adjust the arms if necessary, and drive in the nails.

Place stakes at a 90 degree angle to the post and then nail arm brace to each stake. Use level to establish a true vertical.

Twenty-two choices of fencing

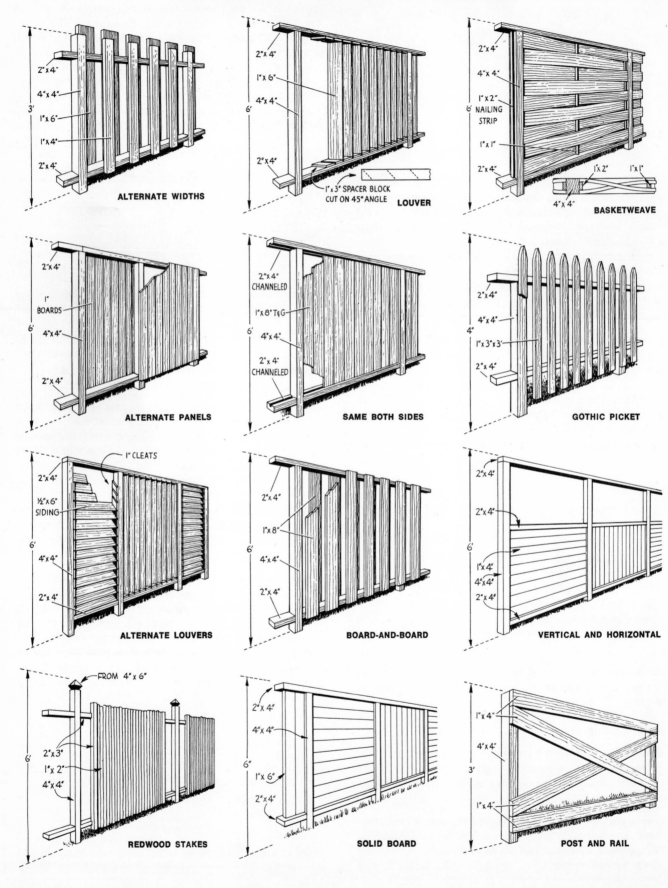

ALTERNATE WIDTHS

2"x 4"
4"x 4"
1"x 6"
1"x 4"
2"x 4"
3'

LOUVER

2"x 4"
1"x 6"
4"x 4"
2"x 4"
6'
1"x 3" SPACER BLOCK CUT ON 45° ANGLE

BASKETWEAVE

2"x 4"
4"x 4"
1"x 2" NAILING STRIP
1"x 1"
2"x 4"
6'
1"x 2"
1"x 1"
4"x 4"

ALTERNATE PANELS

2"x 4"
1" BOARDS
4"x 4"
2"x 4"
6'

SAME BOTH SIDES

2"x 4" CHANNELED
1"x 8" T&G
4"x 4"
2"x 4" CHANNELED
6'

GOTHIC PICKET

2"x 4"
4"x 4"
1"x 3"x 3'
2"x 4"
4"

ALTERNATE LOUVERS

1" CLEATS
2"x 4"
1/2"x 6" SIDING
4"x 4"
2"x 4"
6'

BOARD-AND-BOARD

2"x 4"
1"x 8"
4"x 4"
2"x 4"
6'

VERTICAL AND HORIZONTAL

2"x 4"
2"x 4"
1"x 4"
4"x 4"
2"x 4"
6'

REDWOOD STAKES

FROM 4"x 6"
2"x 3"
1"x 2"
4"x 4"
6'

SOLID BOARD

2"x 4"
4"x 4"
1"x 6"
2"x 4"
6'

POST AND RAIL

1"x 4"
4"x 4"
1"x 4"
3'

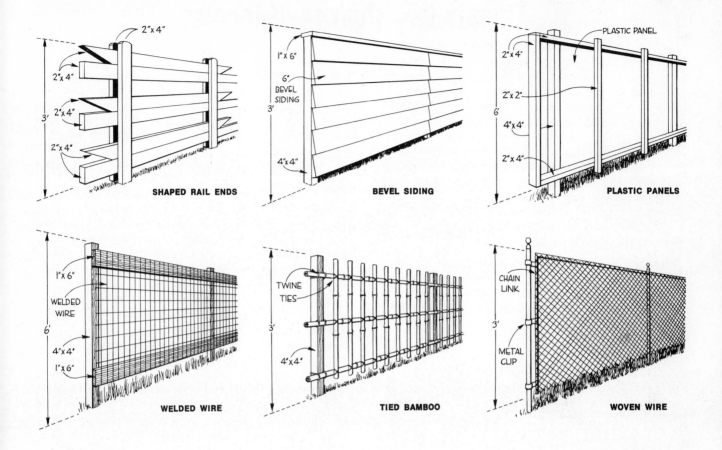

SHAPED RAIL ENDS

2" x 4"
2" x 4"
2" x 4"
2" x 4"
3'

BEVEL SIDING

1" x 6"
6" BEVEL SIDING
4" x 4"
3'

PLASTIC PANELS

PLASTIC PANEL
2" x 4"
2" x 2"
4" x 4"
2" x 4"
6'

WELDED WIRE

1" x 6"
WELDED WIRE
4" x 4"
1" x 6"
6'

TIED BAMBOO

TWINE TIES
4" x 4"
3'

WOVEN WIRE

CHAIN LINK
METAL CLIP
3'

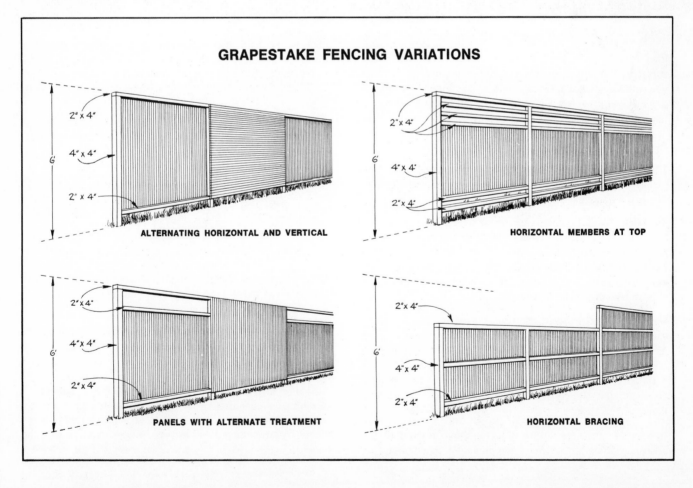

GRAPESTAKE FENCING VARIATIONS

ALTERNATING HORIZONTAL AND VERTICAL

2" x 4"
4" x 4"
2" x 4"
6'

HORIZONTAL MEMBERS AT TOP

2" x 4"
4" x 4'
2" x 4'
6'

PANELS WITH ALTERNATE TREATMENT

2" x 4"
4" x 4"
2" x 4"
6'

HORIZONTAL BRACING

2" x 4'
4" x 4'
2" x 4'
6'

Building a garden gate

To many people a garden gate may be simply a movable part of a fence, convenient for getting through to the other side. Others may think of a gate as something that should be especially attractive, as the focal point of a garden or an invitation to enter. Ornate or simple, all gates must meet one common requirement: They have to work. Just a few miscalculations or a little bad workmanship on a gate, and you end up with one that doesn't close, or worse, one that won't open in wet weather.

How do you go about building a gate from scratch? What are some of the difficulties you're apt to encounter? Here are answers to these and other questions that may arise.

PLAN YOUR DESIGN CAREFULLY

Generally speaking, you put in a gate because you have to get through a fenced area, so its design is normally dictated by that of the fence itself. By using the same materials for both and the same design, you can make the gate blend right into the fence. By altering the design slightly, you can make the gate stand out without creating a sharp contrast with the fence. It's a good

idea to make a sketch of the design you'd like and show it to someone at a lumber yard who knows carpentry. He can tell you whether your plan is feasible, how much it's likely to cost, and whether there is a way to make the job easier by changing the design slightly.

CHOOSING THE MATERIALS

The choice of materials to use for a gate should be based principally on their ability to withstand the weather and the wear and tear a gate gets over the years.

The latch. Although it may seem like putting the cart before the horse, the first thing to consider is the latch. In most cases you have to build the gate around the latch, unless it's a simple hasp or hook and eye. Check with your local hardware and lumber supply stores. They usually carry many different types of latches (see sketches on page 11).

Hinges. The most commonly used hinges are shown in the sketches on page 11. They all have their advantages as well as drawbacks, but any type will do the job if it is big enough and if you use screws and nails that are long enough.

Be sure to select hinges with a weather-resistant coating — cadmium, zinc, or galvanized — unless you plan on painting them; otherwise, they'll rust.

Gate posts. To withstand the weight and pull of the gate, the posts have to be set securely in the ground. Tamped earth may work well for fence posts, but not for gate posts. Set them deep and in concrete (see pages 4 and 5). Use 4 by 4 redwood or cedar as they are more resistant to rot than other woods.

Other grades of wood can be used for gate posts if you treat them with a preservative. Some of the most commonly used preservatives are pentachlorophenol, copper naphthenate, and creosote.

Creosote is fairly effective if properly applied, but has some unpleasant traits that make it unpopular with many gate builders. Principal objection is that the treated area can never be painted over. Many people also object to its heavy, medicinal odor. However, these drawbacks may not be important if you are building a gate in the country or one that is rustic and unpainted in the city.

Pentachlorophenol has an appealing quality to the homeowner because it is clean and odorless. Also, when applied with a clear oil, it leaves no stain. After treatment, evaporation from the treated areas leaves each tiny wood cell wall lined with a permanent elastic film. As a result, the usual cracking and swelling changes which normally take place in aging are fairly well controlled.

Copper napthenate is non-corrosive, therefore eliminating the possibility of injurious effect on plantings. Commonly available in a green color, it may be used as a green stain. Paint may be applied over it, for the color does not come through paint, but it should not be applied over existing paint or varnish.

The method for treating gate posts is simple and inexpensive. Usually only 30 inches of the post is treated, which takes care of 24 inches below the soil and 6 inches above. Before treatment, pierce the post all around the 24-inch mark to allow the preservative solution to soak in even further. Ordinary 50-gallon oil drums can be used as containers for the treating solution.

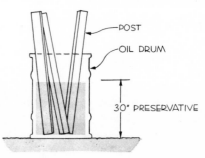

POST

OIL DRUM

30" PRESERVATIVE

After 24 hours of soaking, the post will have an unbroken ring of treated wood, penetrating at least one-half to three-quarters of an inch.

Choosing the lumber. A variety of materials is available for gates. On the West Coast, redwood, cedar, and fir are the most widely used. Under heavy stress, screws and nails may pull out of redwood and cedar more easily than out of fir.

Be sure to check the lumber to see that it isn't warped. It doesn't take much of a curve to throw a whole gate frame out of line. Sometimes you may have to go through a half dozen pieces before getting a straight one. Also check to see if the lumber is seasoned. If it is green, let it dry out for at least a month before you use it. Lay the boards on blocks to let the air circulate freely around the wood. Make sure the blocks hold the boards flat; if they sag, they may warp.

PUTTING THE GATE TOGETHER

Most wood gates have 2 by 4-inch frames covered with some type of siding. You can use lighter frames if the siding is exterior plywood or other light, one-piece paneling material. These won't sag, but they usually need support to keep them from bowing, and to give you a place to fasten hinges and latches.

Assuming you are using the standard 2 by 4 frame and 4 by 4 posts, first measure the distance between the posts (take the measurements both at bottom and top). Leave at least ½ to ¾ inch between the latch post and the gate frame (see sketch below). This allows space for the gate to swing without nicking

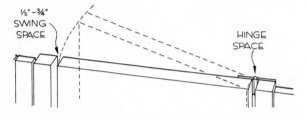

or binding the edge of the post. A tightly fitting gate may look neat, but chances are it won't open easily.

If you're not handy at keeping track of fractions and other measurements, use a straight 1 by 1 garden stake as a guide. Holding it level between the gate posts, mark off the latch post, the ½ to ¾-inch swing space, the gate frame member, hinge space, and the hinge post. You can build the gate frame using this as your only guide.

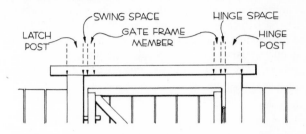

Make sure you cut square corners on all frame members. Check the ends you don't cut, since they're not always cut square at the sawmill. It's always a good idea to drill screw and nail holes. Use a bit that's slightly smaller in diameter than the screw or nail. Include a water-resistant glue on joints when you assemble. Use galvanized or other treated hardware that won't corrode and discolor the wood.

USE THE PROPER BRACING

A gate must be rigid or it will sag. The most commonly used brace is a 2 by 4, set diagonally from the bottom corner of the frame on the hinge post side to the top corner of the latch side. This actually pushes up the frame from the bottom of the hinge

---

STEP-BY-STEP CONSTRUCTION OF A GARDEN GATE

Here is a gate building project for you to follow — from the first step straight through to the self-satisfying stage of opening and closing the gate for the first time.

Before you begin the actual construction of the gate, first measure the distance between the posts at the top and bottom. If the space is not the same, make the posts vertically parallel either by forcing them apart at the top with a brace, or drawing them together with a wire turnbuckle.

Also make sure that you cut square corners on all framing members and check the ends that have been cut at the lumber yard.

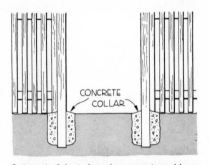

Set posts 2 feet deep in concrete; add concrete collar for extra strength. Width of gate opening is 3½ feet for easy passage.

Fit frame into opening to make sure it lines up with posts. Attach hinges large enough to withstand swing weight of gate.

Mark angle of brace carefully; set in place from bottom of hinge post to top of latch post; secure with nails and glue.

Nail siding to frame using your foot to keep each member vertically straight. Use spacer blocks for evenness in spacing.

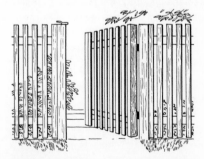

Completed fence swings freely without nicking or binding the edge of latch post. Top latch keeps gate securely closed.

post; you can't do this by running a wood brace the opposite way and expect the gate not to sag.

The inexperienced gate builder will have the hardest time of all getting the brace to fit snugly — and you won't get good support otherwise. Hold the 2 by 4 in place and mark the angle with a pencil. Be sure to use an exact measurement because if you're off ⅛ inch, you won't get a tight fit. If you cut the brace and you find that it doesn't fit snugly, tighten it up with a wedge.

Another good way to brace a gate is to run a wire and turnbuckle or a metal rod diagonally from the top of the frame on the hinge side to the bottom on the latch side (just the opposite of the wooden brace). This brace pulls up the frame to the top of the hinge post. You can buy sets containing wire, a turnbuckle, and two metal angle plates that fit over the edges of the gate frame. Or you can attach the wire to screw eyes set in the frame. You can also have a rod and turnbuckle rig made up at a metal shop.

INSTALLING THE LATCH

Although the latch is the first thing to consider, it's the last thing you put on the gate. If all goes well, the gate should close smoothly and latch securely, and the latch should work easily. Remember that the latch is going to take a heavy beating. A flimsy latch put on with small nails or screws won't hold up for long.

HOW TO FIX A SAGGING GATE

Garden and entry gates normally take a sound beating. They're exposed to the wind and weather and to young garden gate swingers and hurried deliverymen. And they often hang from a fence that is not too rigid a structure and one that tends to expand and contract with the weather. So gates often bind, refuse to latch, or

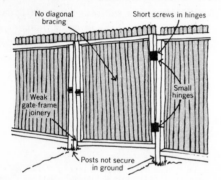

No diagonal bracing · Short screws in hinges · Weak gate-frame joinery · Small hinges · Posts not secure in ground

drag on the ground. If yours has one of these annoyances, here are some ways to eliminate the trouble.

A major cause of trouble is inadequate hinges. Check them — if loose, either replace with larger hinges or replace their screws with longer ones or bolts (most screws that come in hinge sets are too short for gate use). Any gate over 5 feet high or over 3 feet wide really needs three hinges, unless it has two extra heavy ones. If yours has only two weak hinges, you can strengthen the gate with a third hinge of similar type, located between the other two and a bit above the middle point.

A leaning hinge-side post is another problem. It's the one that carries the weight of the gate and of anyone swinging on it. If yours has leaned, you will need to straighten and stiffen it in some

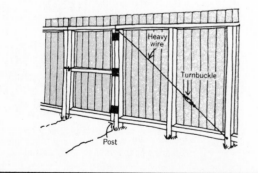

Heavy wire · Turnbuckle · Post

way. Straightening it up and then tamping the soil around it may work — but not always. If it hasn't been concreted in place, it probably should be.

If the hinge post has simply leaned straight over from the weight of the gate, you can straighten and hold it with a turnbuckle and heavy wire or threaded steel rod running to the bottom of another post down the fence line, as shown in the sketch at left below. Do the same to the post on the latch side if it has leaned.

The gate itself is a third major cause of sagging. Most wooden gates aren't overly strong and, subjected to the weather, will sag out of shape. Many good wooden gates have 2 by 4 diagonal braces and are glued together as well as nailed or screwed. For

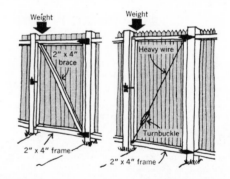

Weight · Weight · 2" x 4" brace · Heavy wire · Turnbuckle · 2" x 4" frame · 2" x 4" frame

others, you can add a wire and turnbuckle on the opposite diagonal to pull the gate back up in place.

Sometimes a gate is given too snug a fit; it works nicely in dry weather but binds when it rains. Plane or cut off some wood to have at least a ¼-inch clearance between the gate and the latch post for expansion in wet weather.

Conversely, a fence with a gate in it may dry out and shrink so much in hot weather that the gate latch will not catch. You need to relocate the latch or replace it with one that has a longer reach.

If your gate has masonry posts and one has tilted slightly, the best answer usually is to trim, shim, or otherwise adjust the gate, leaving the masonry alone. If your masonry post has a considerable tilt, it needs to be plumbed and have more concrete poured around its base.

In some soils, a gate post will sink straight down, particularly if it is of heavy masonry, to a point where the gate latch will not work or the gate drags on the ground. Simply reset the latch or the hinges, whichever is needed.

HARDWARE FOR GARDEN GATES

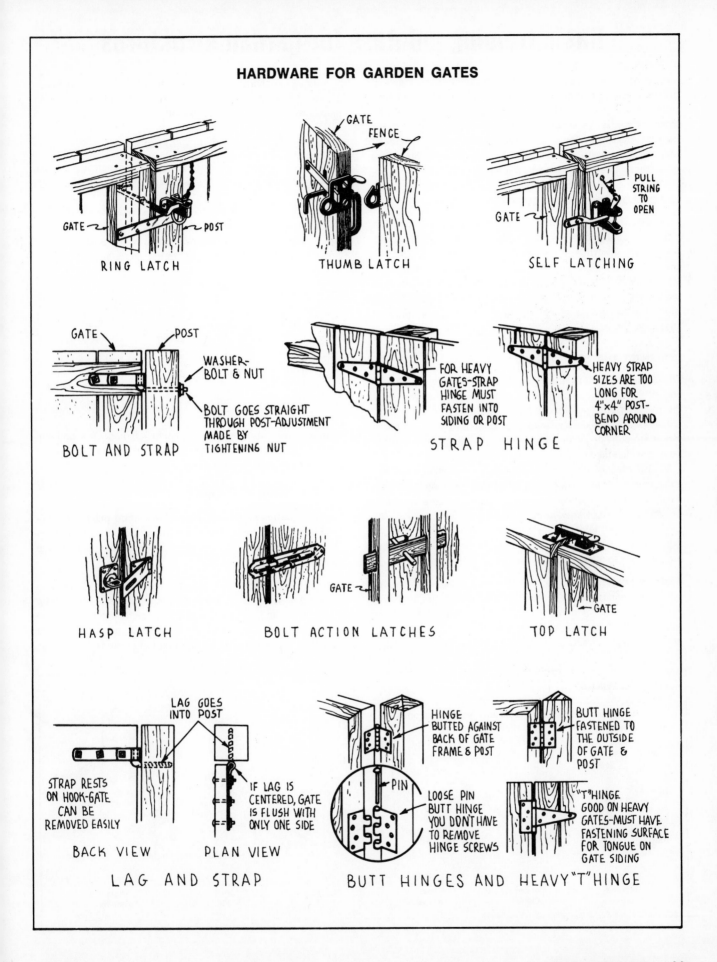

RING LATCH

THUMB LATCH

SELF LATCHING

BOLT AND STRAP

STRAP HINGE

HASP LATCH

BOLT ACTION LATCHES

TOP LATCH

LAG AND STRAP

BUTT HINGES AND HEAVY "T" HINGE

Basic framing pointers for garden structures

Most garden structures are designed to aid the homeowner in caring for plants and flowers; for storing garden tools and supplies; as a shelter against the sun, wind, or rain as an entertainment center; or simply as a place to relax. Whatever the purpose, the discussion below presents some basic methods of building garden structures, and is a guide from the first planning stages through actual construction.

CHECK LOCAL BUILDING CODES

In most communities, you must obtain a building inspector's approval of plans for any kind of outdoor structure. Before starting the job, it's wise to check on setback and height restrictions. Once the plans are finalized, they should be submitted to your local building department for approval. A simple plan sketch showing relationship to property lines, lumber dimensions, framing details, and piers and foundations is normally all that is required.

DESIGNING THE STRUCTURE

The use of any garden structure normally determines its design and location. First planning stages must include decisions as to the need for sun and wind control, plumbing and electricity, and storage. Consideration should also be given to the relation of the structure to other activity areas, buildings, and natural objects which take up space in the garden.

Most outdoor structures, like houses, are essentially rectangular in plan. Many variations are possible involving the same basic construction elements. If you desire a more intricate design, it is wise to seek professional assistance.

The minimum height of any structure should be eight feet, if possible. No matter what type of roof you select, it should be high enough to allow for head clearance in all areas.

Basic roof designs. The flat and shed roof designs are by far the most commonly used for outdoor structures. The gable and pyramid roofs are somewhat more complicated for the do-it-yourselfer to undertake, but they are basic roof designs and most building contractors can handle them with ease.

Although appearance is often the deciding factor in the design of the roof, if the roof is to be watertight, it should be slightly sloped to allow for moisture run-off.

STRUCTURAL ELEMENTS ARE BASIC

Most garden structures are of post and beam design. Posts, properly spaced to provide adequate support, are set in the ground or securely connected to a firm foundation. The posts support horizontal beams which in turn support the roof rafters at right angles to the beams. Some structures can be attached to existing buildings and a modification of the basic post and beam construction is then used. In the sketch below, a ledger

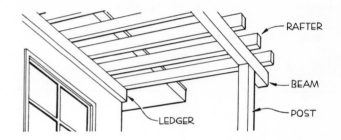

strip is shown attached to an existing building. The building takes the place of posts on one side and the rafters rest directly on the ledger strip.

SETTING POSTS FOR SUPPORT

For most garden structures, 4 by 4 heartwood posts are sufficiently large. For large structures, bigger posts are sometimes necessary to support heavier roof loads and still maintain wide post spacing.

Posts in the ground. The simplest method of anchoring a supporting post is to set it directly in the ground and firmly tamp the earth around the post until it has sufficient rigidity (see figure A below). If soil is sandy or unstable, a concrete collar should be poured around the post on top of the tamped earth.

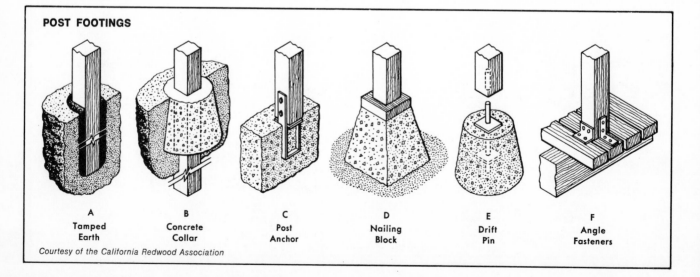

POST FOOTINGS

A	B	C	D	E	F
Tamped Earth	Concrete Collar	Post Anchor	Nailing Block	Drift Pin	Angle Fasteners

Courtesy of the California Redwood Association

The depth to which posts should be set depends on the soil conditions and wind load. 36 inches is adequate for most 8 to 10-foot-high structures.

If you use heartwood posts of redwood, cedar, and other decay-resistant woods, no preservative treatment is usually required before setting the posts directly in the ground but it's helpful. (For a discussion on preservatives for woods, see page 8.)

When supporting posts are set in the ground, the floor of the structure may be a deck, gravel, paving blocks, grass, or earth. Ordinarily, if a concrete slab is to be poured for the floor, the posts are anchored to the slab rather than set in the ground.

Posts on concrete. Three common methods are illustrated in the sketches below. Patented post anchors of many types, available at most local building supply dealers, may be imbedded in the concrete (see figure C). This method provides positive anchorage of the posts to the concrete. The nailing block method (see figure D) allows the post to be toenailed to a redwood block that has been set in concrete.

When a concealed anchorage is desired, the drift pin (figure E) is often used. A moisture barrier — a piece of flat metal or heavy asphalt paper — should be left between the bottom of the post and the concrete surface to avoid the accumulation of moisture and dirt.

If the structure is to be built above an existing deck, the posts may be placed over the existing support members of the deck. The posts should be firmly anchored with angle fasteners (see figure F).

CONNECTING POSTS AND BEAMS

The basic function of roof beams in any structure is to support the rafters and to tie the posts together, producing solid rigidity. To perform these functions properly, the beams must be adequately connected to the posts. Where design permits, the best bearing is achieved when the beam is placed directly on top of the post.

Several methods of connection are possible. A patented post cap (see figure A) is useful where the beam is the same width as the post. Many of these models are commercially available. A wood cleat (see figure B) can also be used in connecting

beams to posts. When the beam is smaller than the width of the post, it may be bolted to a notched post singly (see figure C), or in pairs to an unnotched post (see figure D). If you want to form a column using a pair of posts separated by a spacer block (see figure E), you can bolt the horizontal member (same width as the spacer block) between the two parts of the column.

HOW TO INSTALL THE RAFTERS

Rafters are normally used to support the finished roof but also may be used alone without other elements to create a roof pattern. The method of installing rafters varies with the manner in which they meet the beam. The most widely used method is to have the rafters resting on top of the supporting member and toenailed in place. If you want to use this method but desire a slightly lower roof height, notch the rafters before toenailing them in place.

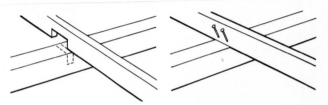

Rafters for either a flat or sloping roof which are to be flush with the top of the beam may be attached in one of several ways: a metal rafter hanger; a wood ledger strip nailed under the rafter for support; or the rafter can be toenailed or nailed from the reverse side of the beam.

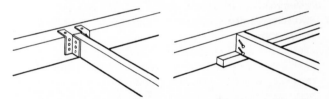

When rafters extend from an existing building, they may be attached either flush or on top of a ledger strip fastened to the building. It is important that the ledger strip be bolted, lag-screwed, or otherwise securely fastened to the existing structure if it is to give the necessary support to the rafters.

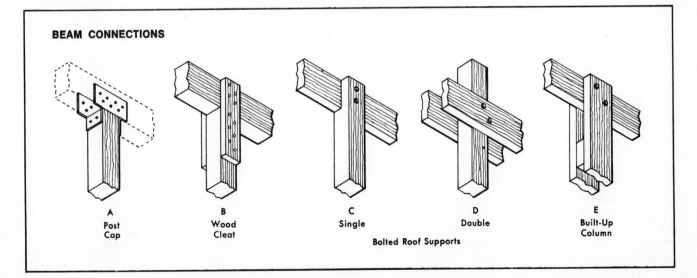

BEAM CONNECTIONS

A	B	C	D	E
Post Cap	Wood Cleat	Single	Double	Built-Up Column

Bolted Roof Supports

Roofing, siding, and flooring for garden structures

Unlike the roof, siding, and flooring for a house, those for a garden structure can usually be quite simple and inexpensive. Most homeowners desire only a reasonably waterproof shelter for garden equipment or a place to relax and entertain during good weather.

YOUR CHOICE IN ROOFING

A shake or shingle roof is a good choice for many garden structures. Either one blends well with trees and plants and has a long life. For a house, many codes require a 4-to-12 pitch on shingles or shakes (4 inches rise to every 12 inches length), but most building inspectors will let you have much less pitch (and thus less roof) on a garden structure, because it is not a living area.

A built-up roof (asphalt and gravel) is also a good choice, particularly for a roof with very little pitch. If you live on a hillside where the roof can be seen from above, consider some attractive colored gravel, rather than the usual grey or black rock.

The corrugated and other fiberglass roofing panels work very well in many garden situations. They are lightweight, require a minimum of support, and are easy to install. They come in a variety of colors and shapes.

Equally good are corrugated and flat panels of asbestos-cement board. These are light-grey in color but can be painted to harmonize with other structures. They last almost indefinitely, are fireproof, and efficiently block off the sun's heat.

On some garden structures, a copper, slate, or tile roof is a very good choice. However, these roofs are comparatively expensive.

For a garden shed, a very low-cost and attractive roof is one made almost flat and covered with 30-pound building felt.

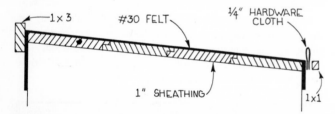

Loose gravel over the felt keeps the sun away — the main thing that deteriorates this inexpensive roofing.

YOUR CHOICE IN SIDINGS

There is a wide variety of house sidings available today which are suitable for garden structures. It is wise to go to a large lumberyard or building materials company and look through their stock and their catalogs before making any choice.

The "standard" house sidings — batten or lapped wood boards, stucco, and masonry veneer — are equally good in a garden. Stucco or masonry needs to be laid up on the job; unless you have had some experience with these materials you should call in a professional. Wood siding is comparatively easy to install yourself, and even easier today because siding boards are available that are exceptionally straight and uniform and factory-primed for painting.

Metal and vinyl sidings are available in various shapes and colors. They need very little maintenance and are very easy to install.

Shingles and shakes make good siding for garden structures and if left to weather naturally, will blend nicely with most landscaping. Applying shingles or shakes as siding is much easier to do than applying them as roofing.

The 4 by 8-foot or larger panels of exterior-grade plywood and hardboard used for siding today go on quickly, and the panels are inexpensive. Many are made with a variety of textured, rough-sawn, and grooved outer surfaces; others are "overlaid" or otherwise given a very smooth surface for painting. You can attach them directly to the studs on a simple garden structure and have a fairly sturdy wall.

Fiberglass and asbestos-cement roofing panels will also give you a lightweight, easily-applied siding for a garden structure. They require practically no maintenance.

YOUR CHOICE IN FLOORING

There's less of a variety of materials to use for floorings suitable for garden structures.

The concrete slab is probably used the most. It's solid, durable, and immune to termites and rot. However, there is considerable work involved in pouring a concrete slab yourself, and if it is laid on soft or adobe soil without adequate steel reinforcing, unsightly cracks may appear in time. A concrete floor can be covered with one of the attractive exterior vinyl floor tiles available today; or with one of the new outdoor carpetings.

Wood floors are particularly adaptable to hillside situations where the floor will be above the ground. Construction is the same as or similar to that of a house floor. Use solid wood planking or *exterior* plywood (most flooring panels are for interior use and will delaminate if exposed to the weather).

All wood members touching the ground should be treated with a preservative. It's also a good idea to eliminate weeds by using a sheet of plastic on the ground under the wood or spraying heavily with a weed killer.

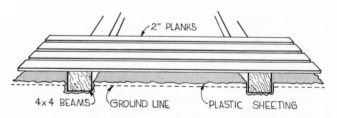

The ready-mix cold asphalt that comes in sacks will make a durable floor for a garden work center, and is one that you can easily lay yourself. For a small area, rent a tamper to do the job; for a large area, use a big lawn roller. (See page 55 for directions.)

Brick or wood blocks can be laid on a sand base for a sturdy garden shelter floor. (See procedure on pages 48 and 49.)

The simplest and most inexpensive flooring is a 4-inch layer of gravel of ½ to ¾-inch size. It drains well and is not difficult to walk on.

HOW TO CONSTRUCT A PATIO OVERHEAD

Building an overhead is not a difficult or complicated task as construction jobs go, but there are points to learn if you want to do it properly. Here is a suggested sequence to follow to help eliminate the possibility of making any serious mistakes — ones that may cause you trouble when the overhead goes into its first winter.

In addition to hammer, saw, and stepladder, you will need a device for establishing level lines. A line-level and 50 feet of chalk line will do nicely, although a carpenter's level can also be used with a long straight board. A 50 or 100-foot tape measure will also prove useful.

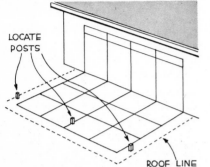

Mark roof line on patio floor with stakes and string. If the roof will be pitched to shed water, don't forget to make allowance for this. Then mark the location of the support posts with stakes or with chalk.

Prepare post footings in one of three ways: in bare ground, dig holes 14 inches deep, 12 inches across; on thick slab, drill hole for metal pin to attach to post; for weak slab, use sledge to dig down 14 inches.

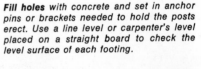

Fill holes with concrete and set in anchor pins or brackets needed to hold the posts erect. Use a line level or carpenter's level placed on a straight board to check the level surface of each footing.

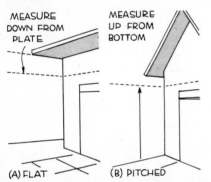

Mark top roof line on house wall measuring (a) down for a patio roof that will run below eaves of the house and (b) up from the foundation for a patio roof that is to be attached to a pitched wall.

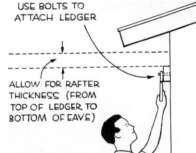

Attach ledger strip to house studs with lag bolts or screws. If the wall is stuccoed, first drill holes with a star drill; if the wall is masonry, drill at least 2 inches into wall and fit in lead sleeves.

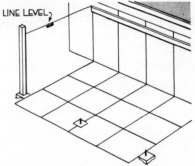

Match post heights to height of ledger strip in this manner: set a post in place and square it up, then run a line-level from top of strip to post, level the line, and mark the post where the line crosses it.

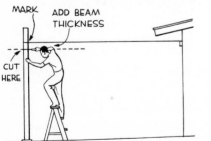

Measure down from the rafter line a distance equal to the thickness of the cross beam and mark a cutting line. Cut off the end of the post at this point. If footings are level, cut other posts to same measurement.

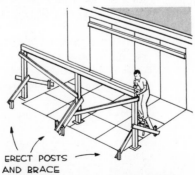

Set all posts, check for vertical alignment, and brace each one with stray pieces of lumber. Then hoist the cross beam on top of the posts, check to see that it is level, and fasten it securely in place.

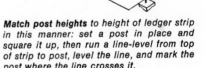
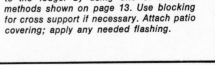

Attach the rafters to the cross beam and to the ledger by using one of the four methods shown on page 13. Use blocking for cross support if necessary. Attach patio covering; apply any needed flashing.

PATIO OVERHEAD CONSTRUCTION 15

Six choices of patio overheads

LACE-ON CANVAS COVERS

The trim nautical look of canvas pulled taut in pipe panels has captured the imagination of many homeowners. Installation is quite simple because tension on the canvas tends to be evenly distributed when it is laced on with a continuous piece of cord. Maintenance is also simple. The canvas can be removed for the winter months with little trouble; tension can be adjusted to keep the panel tight; if you don't mind the sight of the frame, you won't have to dismantle the pipes.

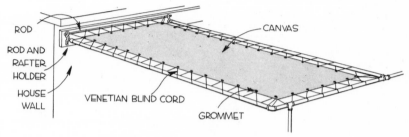

ROD
ROD AND RAFTER HOLDER
HOUSE WALL
VENETIAN BLIND CORD
CANVAS
GROMMET

CORRUGATED PLASTIC PANELS

Of the various materials available, corrugated plastic panels are the most widely used for overheads. The most popular corrugated panel is 26 inches wide, which provides for a 2-inch overlap and installation on rafters spaced 2 feet on centers. Ideal installation for these panels is over a framework that has rafters spaced 2 feet apart with the corrugations running lengthwise. If cutting is necessary, use a fine-toothed handsaw or a power saw with an abrasive blade.

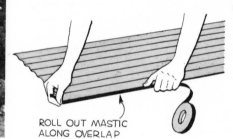

ROLL OUT MASTIC ALONG OVERLAP

USE CORRUGATED-ROOFING NAILS

EGGCRATE OVERHEAD GIVES FEELING OF PROTECTION

Open to the sky, but substantial enough to give a sheltered feeling, the eggcrate overhead may be the answer to your particular situation. An added advantage is that this shelter can be covered with another material to provide more shade and protection. Once the basic framing members are in place, all you have to do is nail in blocking between the rafters. Carefully measure the distance between the rafters and saw blocking to fit snugly. Use four nails to secure each end, two on each side.

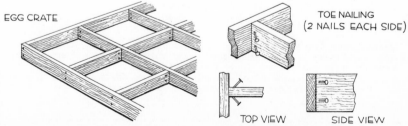

EGG CRATE

TOE NAILING (2 NAILS EACH SIDE)

TOP VIEW

SIDE VIEW

LATH SHELTERS CAN BE PERMANENT OR REMOVABLE

Inexpensive, easy to install, and adaptable enough to provide you with as little or as much protection as any other cover, lath deserves consideration for any overhead where water tightness is not a requirement. You can build panels which can be removed from the framework or you can nail lath to the frame and make it permanent. The sketch below shows how you can get uniform, parallel spacing between lath strips using a spacer. Use two nails on each end of each lath.

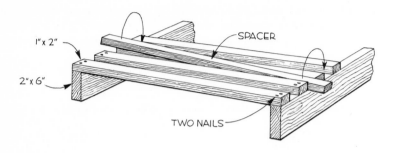

REED IS INEXPENSIVE AND EASY TO HANDLE

Lightweight, with interesting textures, a woven reed overhead requires a minimum understructure. It is also easier to install than almost any other material. Because the material is so light, it can be laid on wires stretched tightly between rafters. If you want the reed to be permanent and able to withstand the elements, use a stapling gun to attach it to the frames, then secure it with 1-inch strips laid on top and wired to the steel wire underneath.

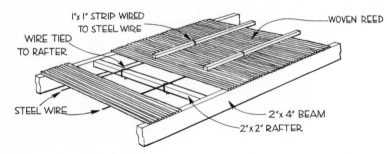

ALUMINUM SCREENING RESISTS CORROSION

Consisting of plastic-coated aluminum wires, aluminum screening attached to an overhead frame not only resists corrosion but helps to reduce sun penetration. It can be installed in various widths. The width you buy will be determined largely by the dimensions of the framework you build, principally the distance between the rafters. Although you may be tempted to install a broad width, you might find it difficult to install without its sagging. The wide screen is hard to pull taut.

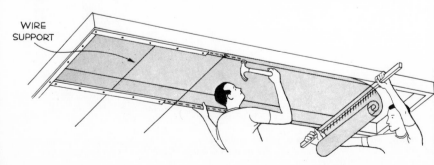

Trellises and frames for plant support

There are many reasons why a young shrub or vine needs more support than just what a stake can give. The crossbarred structure of a trellis offers more width and more places to tie a sprawling plant. When a plant is splayed out in graceful curves and masses against a background grid, it often looks better and displays its flowers or fruits better than when it's allowed to grow freely in all directions.

A framework that holds a plant away from a wall also keeps it healthier. Good air circulation minimizes mildew and rot.

Rampant growers like ivy can benefit by the discipline of a sturdy trellis. A strong framework offers the vine some alterna-

tive to filling every crack and crevice in the fence or wall, and it encourages a gardener to keep the vine trimmed back. (Almost any plant when grown on a trellis needs more pruning and pinching than when grown elsewhere.)

Finally, the trellis structure itself adds all-year interest to a fence or a blank house wall. This is especially true if it provides some color contrast; for example, a dark-stained framework against a light-colored wall (or vice versa), or glistening white latticework set into a dark green fence.

The twelve examples below and on the next page show the great variety of trellises that you can build.

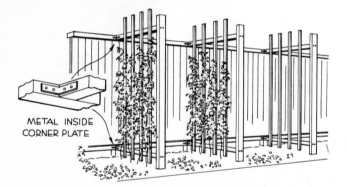

Two or three arches *give a bowerlike effect. Use 2 by 2 posts attaching cross strips to width you desire.*

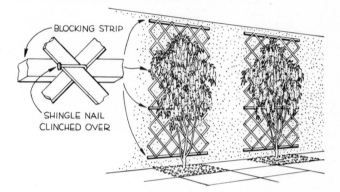

Prefab sections *of 2 by 4-foot trellises are placed end to end. Block out from the house or garage with 2 by 2-inch strips.*

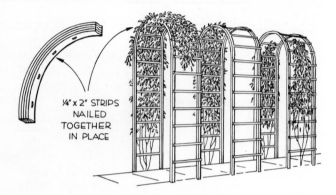

Wing trellis *is the most effective in multiples. Nail beanpoles or bamboo to the frame of 2 by 4's or 3 by 4's.*

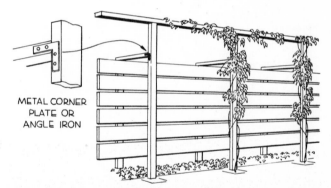

An open frame *of redwood 2 by 4's is set out from an existing fence and can rise above it to any height that is locally legal.*

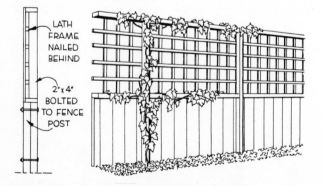

Fence raiser *for a low fence that could go higher is made so that its frame accommodates ready-made, see-through trellis.*

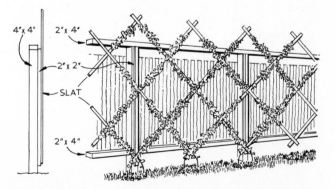

For easy espalier, *apply 1 by 2 or 2 by 2-inch strips (painted a contrasting color) to the fence; train plants up the diagonals.*

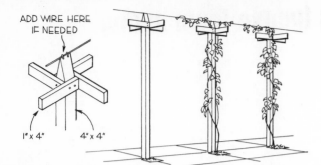

Artificial tree *could display a grape, wisteria, gourd vine, special rose, or honeysuckle to scent the garden; can be any height.*

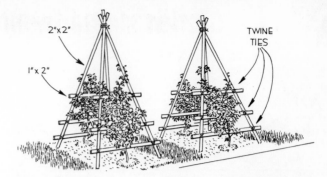

Pyramid for tomatoes *provides good air circulation and shades the root area. Use beanpoles, grape stakes, or scrap lumber.*

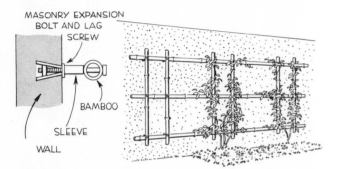

Bamboo *used in the Japanese style is fastened with lag screws. You could lash with copper wire or with heavy cord, instead.*

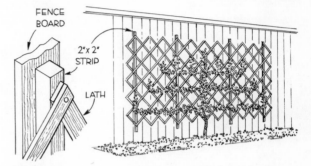

Espalier frame *is standard trellis (4 by 8 feet) held away from the fence by wood strips. Fasten with clinched-over nails.*

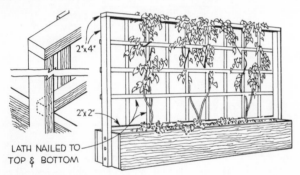

Free-standing screen *is mounted in ordinary type of planter; makes good patio privacy screen, space divider, or windbreak.*

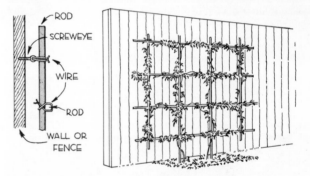

Unbreakable trellis *is made with steel reinforcing rods wired together, then attached to the wall with screw eyes or eyebolts.*

USEFUL HARDWARE FOR SUPPORTING VINES

The special hardware shown below solves most problems in attaching vines or trellises to wood, masonry, and plaster walls. Drill holes in masonry with a star or carbide tip drill.

Once you have the basic hardware up, the kind of tie you select will depend on the weight and vigor of the vine, how it grows, and the kind of structure that's supporting it.

For a lightweight twining vine, use soft twine, raffia, wide rubber bands, or plastic or reinforced paper ties. For heavy-stemmed vines, particularly those that have no way of holding on, use heavier, longer lasting materials such as pliable, insulated wire, heavy rubber tree ties, sections of clothesline (woven cotton or plastic-covered), or strips of canvas.

Check ties frequently, replace or loosen them if necessary, and add new ties as growth progresses.

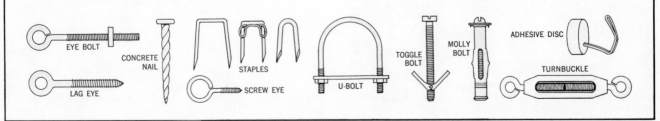

Garden shelter with a deluxe lawn swing

A simple structure, this garden shelter is called an "instant shade tree" by its designer. It is especially useful in areas where the summer gets hot and in small gardens.

Design: Marc Askew.

Deluxe lawn swing hung from rafters adds an interesting focal point to a garden that is considerably wider than it is deep.

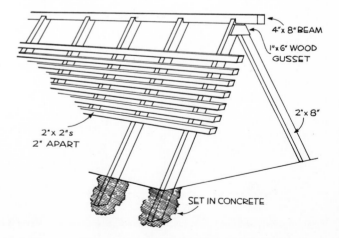

PRIMARY FRAMING VIEW

- 2"x 6" RIDGE BEAM
- 18'
- 2 - 2"x 6" LINTELS
- 6"x 6" POSTS
- 9' 3"
- 9' 6"
- 3'

END VIEW

- 1"x 12" ROOF SHEATHING
- CEDAR SHAKE ROOF
- 2"x 6" FASCIA
- 2"x 4" RAFTER
- 4"x 4" PLATE
- 2"x 6" LINTELS
- 2"x 6" BEAMS
- 1"x 2" TRIM
- 2 - ½"x 12" BOLTS
- 6"x 6"x 12' POST
- CREOSOTE BOTTOM 3' OF POST, STUD WITH 16d GALV· NAILS AND SET IN CONCRETE

Redwood A-frame shelter

A quiet place for a few moments alone, this geometric A-frame structure shelters from both the sun and wind.

The basic framework is 2 by 8 redwood support beams set in concrete with a 4 by 8 ridge beam. The sides are 2 by 2's evenly spaced. The wood can be painted, stained, or left natural.

Although the floor shown in the photograph is brick laid in sand, any other type of garden structure flooring could be used (see page 14).

Design: Armand Ramirez.

- 4"x 8" BEAM
- 1"x 6" WOOD GUSSET
- 2"x 8"
- 2"x 2"s 2" APART
- SET IN CONCRETE

Octagonal gazebo with storage area

This octagonal gazebo is only 11 feet in diameter, but in half of it there is room for swimming pool equipment and two dressing rooms; the other half forms a sun-protected outdoor room.

The open-beam roof is supported by eight 4½-inch diameter pipes sunk into the exposed aggregate flooring of the terrace. The walls and doors are ¾-inch exterior plywood, painted white; the fanciful top-knot, a vent for the pool heater, is copper, treated with acid to make it turn green, and topped with a copper float of the type used in a toilet tank.

Architect: Morgan Stedman.

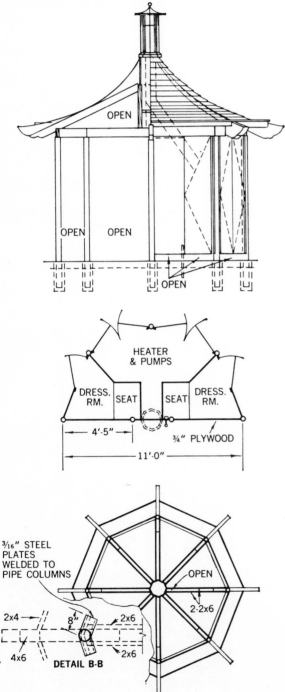

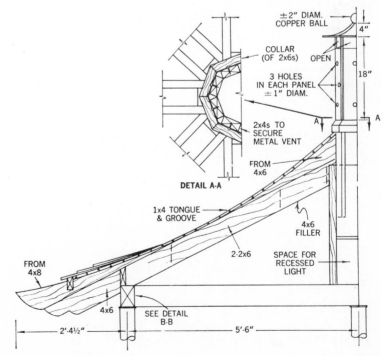

Tiny, white gazebo overlooks pool from upper terrace where it also provides a semicircle of shade for warm afternoons.

Entertainment pavilion by the pool

As a shelter for entertaining or relaxing, or as a shelter in which children can "camp out" in the summer, this pavilion adjacent to the house and swimming pool is as delightful as it is functional.

In design, building materials, and colors, the pavilion ties in beautifully with the house located about 35 feet away. The roof is built of ⅝-inch exterior plywood covered with sheet metal. The wedge-shaped sections are painted soft blue, gray-green, ochre, and white. Undersides of the pavilion roof are soft blue.

Sleeping bags and other equipment are kept in a three-sectioned storage bench (with a lid) inside the pavilion at the rear. Canvas curtains can be pulled when necessary to shut out the sun or wind.

A light fixture hangs from the pavilion ceiling. Waterproof outlets are available for electric cooking equipment and additional night lighting. The pavilion is particularly charming when lighted at night.

Design: Roy Rydell.

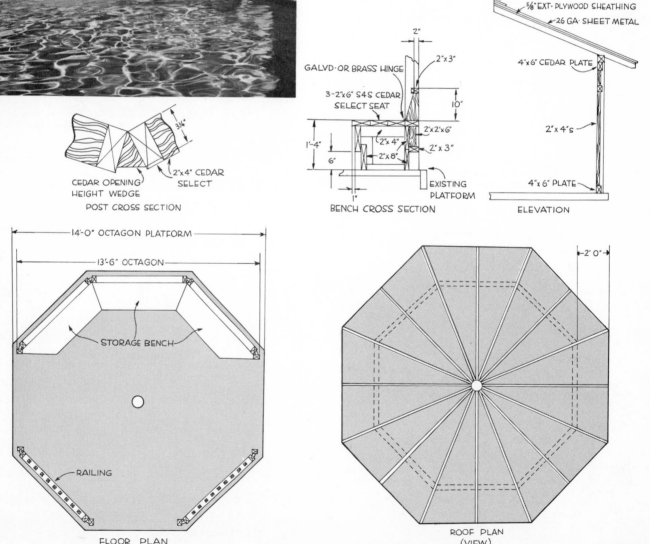

CEDAR OPENING HEIGHT WEDGE
2"x4" CEDAR SELECT
POST CROSS SECTION

GALVD·OR BRASS HINGE
3-2"x6" S4S CEDAR SELECT SEAT
2"x3"
10"
2"x2"x6"
2"x4"
2"x3"
1'-4"
2"x8"
6"
1"
EXISTING PLATFORM
BENCH CROSS SECTION

GALVD·CAP
⅝" EXT·PLYWOOD SHEATHING
26 GA· SHEET METAL
4"x6" CEDAR PLATE
2"x4"s
4"x6" PLATE
ELEVATION

14'-0" OCTAGON PLATFORM
13'-6" OCTAGON
STORAGE BENCH
RAILING
FLOOR PLAN

2' 0"
ROOF PLAN (VIEW)

Redwood lattice-work gazebo

Constructed of durable redwood, this jaunty and whimsical gazebo was patterned after the "meditation retreats" that were so popular during the Victorian era.

The drawing below indicates how the wrought iron effect was achieved by stringing ⅜-inch redwood slats and spacer blocks on a ¼-inch galvanized metal rod.

Architect: Germano Milono.

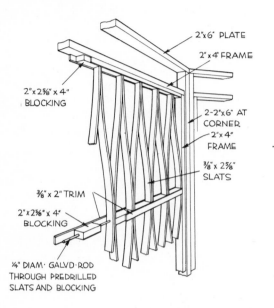

2"x6" PLATE

2" x 4" FRAME

2" x 2⅝" x 4" BLOCKING

2-2"x6" AT CORNER

2" x 4" FRAME

⅜" x 2⅝" SLATS

⅜" x 2" TRIM

2" x 2⅝" x 4" BLOCKING

¼" DIAM· GALVD·ROD THROUGH PREDRILLED SLATS AND BLOCKING

Versatile and portable pavilions

These portable garden pavilions can be used in a variety of ways: as party pavilions, playhouses for children, or as a shaded place for plants. One will liven up a garden or pool area; if you have several, you can treat them as modular units or as separate little rooms. You might put three together over a long dining table, or set units in separate corners of a garden.

The pavilions are proportioned so that each uses a 4 by 10-foot panel of ⅛-inch tempered hardboard with no waste except for the cut-out arches. Frames — legs and top crosspieces — are finished 2 by 2's.

White pine was used for the pavilions shown in the photograph, but redwood, cedar, and fir are just as suitable and cost less. To cover the top, you can use fiberglass shade screening, canvas, woven reed, or flat plastic panels.

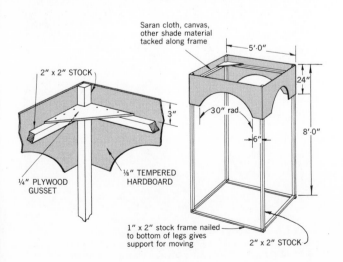

2" x 2" STOCK

Saran cloth, canvas, other shade material tacked along frame

5'-0"

24"

3"

30" rad.

6"

8'-0"

¼" PLYWOOD GUSSET

⅛" TEMPERED HARDBOARD

1" x 2" stock frame nailed to bottom of legs gives support for moving

2" x 2" STOCK

More ideas for garden shelters

Shelter is enclosed on two windward sides with panels of hardboard and 10 removable windows. The trellislike overhead is covered with 2 by 2's for filtered shade. Design: Louis Kapranos.

Five-sided shelter has wide entry and low seating around the four sides. The roof is partly shingled and partly opened to give both shade and free air movement. Design: Marc Askew.

Airy garden pavilion consists of framework of upright horizontal members that suggests an enclosure while remaining open. Bench stretches across rear side. Design: Jack W. Buktenica.

Sides of pavilion are open to catch the slightest breeze and to make the structure part of the garden. The floor is of red brick, top is covered with panels of canvas. Design: Anthony Silvers.

Building a garden bench

With the variety of garden furniture that you can buy ready made, why build a garden bench? The most obvious reason is to gain a piece of garden furniture that is tailor-made. Another good reason is adaptability. At times a garden bench may become a garden shelf for the display of plants in containers or a piece of driftwood. In certain locations, as at the end of a deck or beside a steep bank, a bench can function as a barrier. Put a back rest on the bench and it's a fence as well. The eight examples shown on the next two pages give you an idea of the many types of benches people are building today.

DESIGN IS HIGHLY INDIVIDUAL

Since most people want to experiment, improvise, and modify the design of a garden bench until it suits their particular surroundings, there is no one basic form to keep in mind. There are, however, a few considerations for comfort and usability.

Height. For maximum comfort a bench should be between 15 and 18 inches high, the approximate height of most chairs. You can make it lower if you plan to use a thick mat or cushion. If you plan to use it primarily for sunbathing, then it can be as low as 6 to 8 inches.

Width. There is no set guide. The width will depend on how you plan to use the bench. However, a bench less than a foot wide isn't very inviting and is apt to look more like a perch than a place to relax. Many gardeners make their benches large enough to accommodate a 24-inch lounge pad. For a combination bench and table, build it 36 to 48 inches wide.

CHOOSING THE LUMBER

Redwood, pine, cedar, fir, and cypress are the woods most frequently used for outdoor benches. Builders and owners of benches stress the importance of using the best grade of lumber for the upper surface of the bench. Well seasoned lumber, without loose knots, will keep its shape and last much longer than that of poorer quality.

Use 2-inch-thick lumber on bench tops for strength. You can also use 1 by 2's or 1 by 3's if you set them on edge, as shown in the step-by-step series below. If you do use wide lumber, such as 2 by 8's or 2 by 10's, it's important that it be well seasoned; otherwise, there's a good chance the planks will warp and split. Be sure to leave about ¼ to ½-inch space between the boards making up the top of the bench to allow for expansion, and for rain water to drain through.

ANCHORING THE BENCH

Bench legs should be sturdy enough for solid support and still be in scale with the rest of the bench. A good idea is to plan the bench to be sturdy; then build it just a little stronger.

Space the legs about 3 to 5 feet apart, closer if you use light legs (such as 2 by 4's) or if the lumber used for the top of the bench is narrow and needs more support to keep from sagging.

STEP-BY-STEP CONSTRUCTION OF A CURVED BENCH

Many amateur craftsmen have undoubtedly approached the task of building a garden bench with a certain amount of trepidation. However, once they got going, they found that the actual step-by-step construction presented few problems.

In the sketches here, you see how one homeowner went about it. He wanted a curved bench that would border a patio and also tie in with a straight walkway that led to the house. His project encompassed most of the complications possible in bench-building.

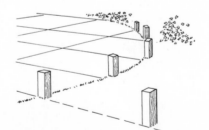

Set posts (4 x 4's) in arc with 30-foot radius, sunk in 18 inches of concrete. Post height above ground is 15½ inches.

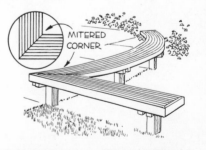

Cut notches into the post tops to take 2 x 4 braces 18 inches long. Bolted to the post, they protrude ½ inch above.

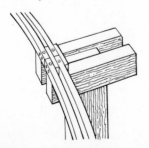

Nail slats (1 x 2-inch) to brace, to oppose bow-like spring of stressed wood. The ½-inch blocks keep spacing uniform.

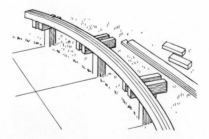

Curve slat to follow arc and nail the other end firmly in place to the next brace. Repeat the procedure for each slat.

Set mitered 1 x 2 at either end to complete bench construction. Use galvanized nails throughout to prevent staining wood.

The photographs on these two pages show various ways to support and brace a bench.

Wood is the most commonly used material for bench legs because it is easy to work with and is less expensive than most other materials. However, you can use 1¼ or 1½-inch pipe, angle iron, flat iron, channel iron, brick, concrete block, or flue tile. All of these materials are rot and termite proof, but they generally take more skill to install and are more expensive than wood.

USE GALVANIZED HARDWARE

To prevent staining of the wood, use only galvanized or non-rusting nails, screws, and bolts. Your hardware or lumber dealer will advise you on the kinds and sizes to buy. It's a good idea to countersink nails and screws so they won't catch on

AROUND A TREE

Outer edge of bench is supported by 2½-inch pipe; inner supports, 4 x 4's. Outside measurement is 7 feet square. Design: Casey Kawamoto.

SUPPORTED BY STEEL

Portable benches are 6 feet long, 2 feet wide. Legs are ¼ x 4-inch flat iron painted black. Top pieces are spaced an inch apart. Design: Paul Weissich.

WITH A RAISED BED

Bracing of two beveled 2 x 8's is fastened to 4 x 4 posts with carriage bolts. Part of bench is attached to retaining wall. Design: Kathryn Imlay Stedman.

ON A GENTLE CURVE

A 40-foot-long bench is supported on 2 x 12's with 2 x 4 bracing. Top is made of 2 x 2's. Bench is by the swimming pool. Design: John Carmack.

clothing. Pre-bore screw and bolt holes, making a wider seat for the screw or bolt head. Countersink nails with a nail set. Fill the holes, if desired, with a non-oily filler, unless you plan to paint the bench. Oily fillers tend to discolor the wood.

A FINISH IS OPTIONAL

Once your bench is completed, you may want to apply a finish. Some bench owners prefer to let the wood weather naturally while others prefer to finish with a sealer, stain, or paint.

Check with your local paint dealer for the various wood finishes available. Be sure you tell him what you want the finish for and emphasize that you want one that won't get tacky in the sun or one that is slow drying.

First try some of the finish on a piece of wood left over from the bench top. Use a piece that's large enough to give you a good idea of what the color and finish will be like.

WITH A GLASS WINDBREAK

The slanted back rest is detachable so the wall can be painted. Glass sections stop the wind, but don't obstruct view. Design: Warren Lauesen.

WITH WEATHERPROOF MATS

Cedar benches 14 inches high, covered with 2-inch-thick, weatherproof mats. Metal legs painted black; ends bolted to concrete. Design: Allen Vance Salsbury.

TIED IN WITH OVERHEAD

Post supporting the patio overhead is also part of 15-foot-long bench. Bracing is hidden from view by 1 x 4 fascia. Top is 2 x 6's. Design: Gil Rovianek.

LOW BENCH RESTS ON CONCRETE

Legs for bench are 4 x 8 x 16-inch concrete blocks. End metal U straps sunk in hollow core of blocks. Top is bolted to straps. Design: Frederick E. Emmons.

Greenhouses you can assemble yourself

The six sketches below indicate the wide choice of designs now available in small, pre-fabricated greenhouses which can be easily assembled by the homeowner. The time required for assembly depends on the type of construction and the size of the structure. Most of them require only a few standard tools. (For more information on where to find them, check the yellow pages of your telephone directory, your local nursery, or builder's supply store.)

POINTS TO CONSIDER

When you begin shopping for a greenhouse, you will want to consider these factors:

Size. Greenhouses range in size from a 3 by 6-foot structure through the standard 9 by 12-foot amateur's model and on up to commercial sizes. Whatever size house you choose, always give a thought to its potential for expansion. Additional sections, 2 to 3 feet wide, are available to expand most of the models illustrated here.

Wood or metal frame. Whether you select a wood, steel, or aluminum frame depends largely on how much money you want to invest. The average life of a redwood frame is 20 years or more. A steel greenhouse painted often enough to keep it from rusting will last indefinitely. An aluminum greenhouse will do the same with little or no maintenance.

Glass vs. plastic. Although glass is still the most widely used of the greenhouse glazing materials, some greenhouse experts feel that fiberglass will replace glass for greenhouse construction within the next few years. It's more resistant to breakage and makes construction cheaper.

Pitch of the roof. A greenhouse roof needs a vertical rise of 6 inches per 12 horizontal inches to handle the run-off from condensation on the glass. If the covering is polyethylene, you can reduce condensation by stretching muslin over the rafters before putting on the covering.

Ventilation and heating. Be sure the greenhouse you buy has some kind of vent for air circulation. Also be sure to have some kind of auxiliary heat if temperatures should drop below freezing in the winter. Small gas or electric heaters are adequate in most cases.

Curved design of roof is more expensive than angular frame. Cement block, brick, or stone sides are also more expensive.

Workshop-greenhouse combination has 10 x 13 ft. of growing area and a 7 x 10-ft. work room; example includes benches.

Plastic panels cover a lightweight wood frame on this easy-to-build structure. Plans available where the plastic is sold.

Lean-to frame is used for a long, narrow area against a building. Used as extension of house. Best with south exposure.

Aluminum frame has been pre-glazed. The structure has 10 sides, and comes 7, 8, or 10 feet in diameter.

A-frame has panels of corrugated plastic. Construction details available where plastic sold. Vented at top, door at one end.

A quonset-style greenhouse

Resembling a gothic arch in shape, this greenhouse can be covered with plastic to shed water and snow and resist wind. In late summer the greenhouse can be used as a propagating frame simply by replacing the plastic cover with a lath-type snow fence.

Two small ventilators located at the top of the doors at each end provide limited ventilation. For added ventilation on warm days, the doors can be opened or the house can be raised off the ground.

Construction is simple requiring only a little experience with common tools.

Design: United States Department of Agriculture.

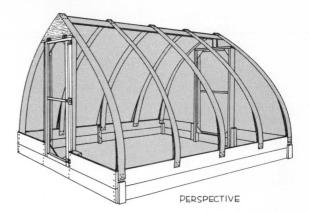

PERSPECTIVE

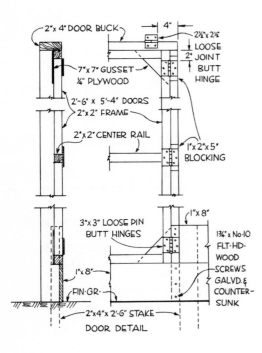

2"x 4" DOOR BUCK

4"

2½"x 2½" LOOSE JOINT BUTT HINGE

2"

7"x 7" GUSSET ¼" PLYWOOD

2'-6" x 5'-4" DOORS

2"x 2" FRAME

2"x 2" CENTER RAIL

1"x 2"x 5" BLOCKING

3"x 3" LOOSE PIN BUTT HINGES

1"x 8"

1¾" x No. 10 FLT·HD· WOOD SCREWS GALVD.& COUNTER-SUNK

1"x 8"

FIN·GR·

2"x4" x 2'-6" STAKE

DOOR DETAIL

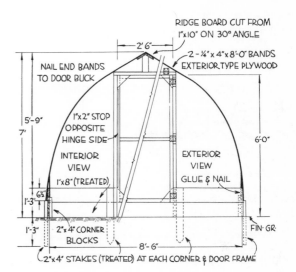

RIDGE BOARD CUT FROM 1"x10" ON 30° ANGLE

2'-6"

2 - ¼" x 4" x 8'-0" BANDS EXTERIOR TYPE PLYWOOD

NAIL END BANDS TO DOOR BUCK

5'-9"

7'

1"x 2" STOP OPPOSITE HINGE SIDE

INTERIOR VIEW

1"x 8" (TREATED)

6'-0"

EXTERIOR VIEW

GLUE & NAIL

6½"

1'-3"

1'-3"

2"x 4" CORNER BLOCKS

FIN·GR·

8'-6"

2"x 4" STAKES (TREATED) AT EACH CORNER & DOOR FRAME

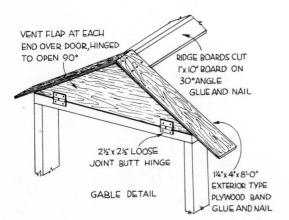

VENT FLAP AT EACH END OVER DOOR, HINGED TO OPEN 90°

RIDGE BOARDS CUT 1"x 10" BOARD ON 30° ANGLE GLUE AND NAIL

2½"x 2½" LOOSE JOINT BUTT HINGE

1¼" x 4" x 8'-0" EXTERIOR TYPE PLYWOOD BAND GLUE AND NAIL

GABLE DETAIL

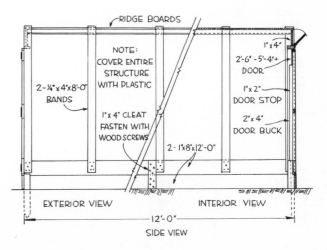

RIDGE BOARDS

NOTE: COVER ENTIRE STRUCTURE WITH PLASTIC

1"x 4"

2'-6" - 5'-4"+ DOOR

1"x 2" DOOR STOP

2"x 4" DOOR BUCK

2 - ¼" x 4" x 8'-0" BANDS

1"x 4" CLEAT FASTEN WITH WOOD SCREWS

2 - 1"x 8"x 12'-0"

EXTERIOR VIEW

INTERIOR VIEW

12'-0"

SIDE VIEW

Simple lean-to greenhouse

If you are handy with tools, you can build and alter the size and shape of this simple lean-to greenhouse to suit your garden and gardening habits. However, before you make too many changes, figure out how your bench layout will go. The usefulness of any greenhouse can be measured by the square feet of bench space. Be sure to install the bench at a convenient height, and don't be afraid to make it as deep as possible.

The footing should be solid, with a level, flat surface at least 4 inches wide. It could be gravel, bricks or stones mortared together, or concrete.

For the frame, use lumber that is dry and straight or the lightweight building will sag. Either redwood or cedar makes good greenhouse framing. The 2 by 4-inch roof support beam holds the glass bearers evenly spaced, and helps to prevent any sag. Notch the horizontal glass bearers as indicated in the sketch, so that water condensing on the underside of the glass can run down, instead of dripping from the ceiling.

Design: Don Round.

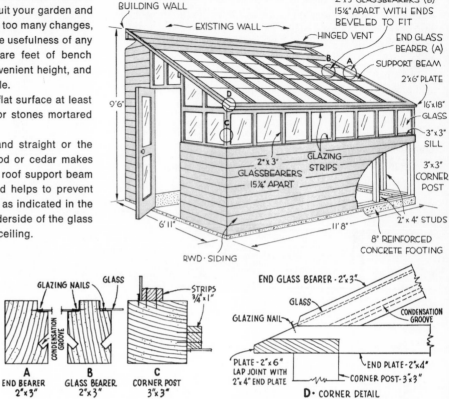

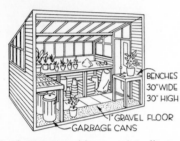

Bench tops *are wide enough to fit standard nursery flats, high enough to provide storage space for pots, mix, unused flats.*

Glass cross-section. *The angular cuts in glass bearers act as gutters for condensation. Use single strength "B" glass.*

Use glazing nails *or ¾-inch galvanized tacks to hold the lower edge of the glass. Overlap each sheet 2 inches.*

A portable greenhouse

This unusual greenhouse is portable and measures 32 inches by 68 inches at the base — large enough to house three dozen orchid plants. Mounted on a frame comparable to a hand truck, it can be wheeled from place to place in the garden. Detachable lath racks are attached to the ridge of the house to provide additional shade.

Design: Dr. Robert A. Kennelly.

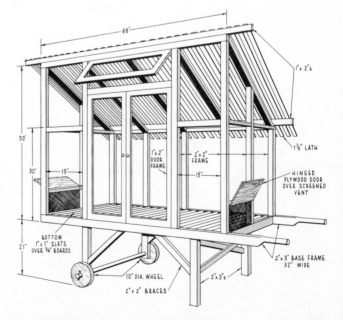

Side and back view. *Two small vents at the bottom, on opposite sides, and one at the top provide adequate ventilation.*

Construction *is quite simple, involving primarily a sturdy frame of 2 by 3-inch redwood to which legs, floor, roof are attached.*

Combination greenhouse-coldframe

This combination greenhouse-coldframe unit is built of 2 by 2 framing members. Use a preservative or paint on all framing members after cutting. The upper section is connected to the lower section with ⅜-inch carriage bolts with wing nuts. The completed unit is anchored to the ground with steel rods and covered with clear polyethylene plastic of 4 mil thickness. If you need only a coldframe, just build the top section and anchor to the ground in the same fashion.

Design: United States Department of Agriculture.

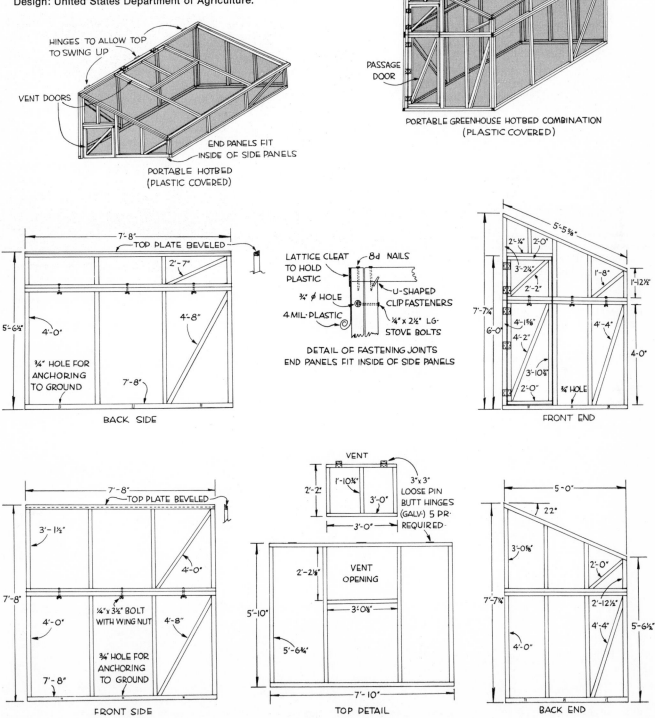

PORTABLE GREENHOUSE HOTBED COMBINATION
(PLASTIC COVERED)

PORTABLE HOTBED
(PLASTIC COVERED)

DETAIL OF FASTENING JOINTS
END PANELS FIT INSIDE OF SIDE PANELS

BACK SIDE

FRONT END

FRONT SIDE

TOP DETAIL

BACK END

Inexpensive hotbed and propagating frame

Inexpensive and easy to build, this hotbed can also be used as a propagating frame. Made chiefly of wood, it has three arch frames of thin-wall electrical conduit. The frames may be easily bent to shape with a conduit bender. Use two covers of polyethylene plastic, attaching them to opposite sides of the ridge beam.

Design: United States Department of Agriculture.

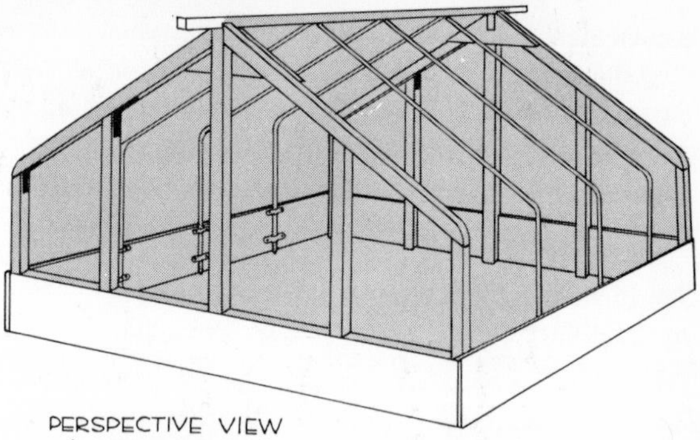

PERSPECTIVE VIEW
(FRAMING ONLY)

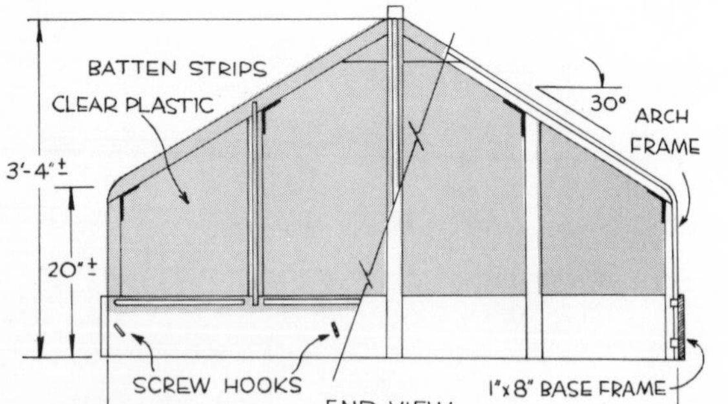

BATTEN STRIPS
CLEAR PLASTIC
30° ARCH FRAME
3'-4"±
20"±
SCREW HOOKS
END VIEW
1"x8" BASE FRAME

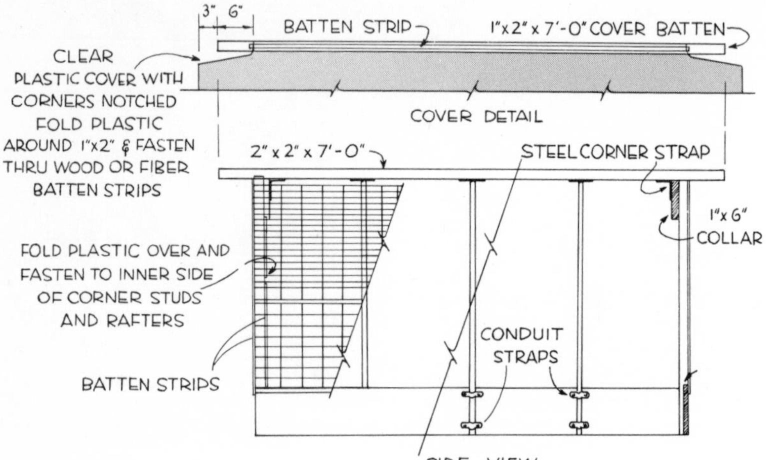

3" 6"
BATTEN STRIP
1"x2" x 7'-0" COVER BATTEN
CLEAR PLASTIC COVER WITH CORNERS NOTCHED FOLD PLASTIC AROUND 1"x2" & FASTEN THRU WOOD OR FIBER BATTEN STRIPS
COVER DETAIL
2"x2" x 7'-0"
STEEL CORNER STRAP
1"x6" COLLAR
FOLD PLASTIC OVER AND FASTEN TO INNER SIDE OF CORNER STUDS AND RAFTERS
BATTEN STRIPS
CONDUIT STRAPS
SIDE VIEW
(CUTAWAY)

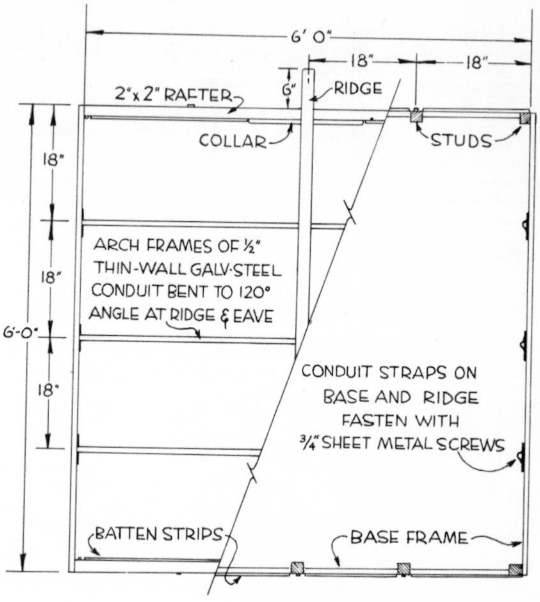

6' 0"
18" 18"
2"x2" RAFTER
6"
RIDGE
COLLAR
STUDS
18"
ARCH FRAMES OF ½" THIN-WALL GALV·STEEL CONDUIT BENT TO 120° ANGLE AT RIDGE & EAVE
18"
6'-0"
CONDUIT STRAPS ON BASE AND RIDGE FASTEN WITH ¾" SHEET METAL SCREWS
18"
BATTEN STRIPS
BASE FRAME
TOP VIEW
(CUT AWAY)

All-season coldframe

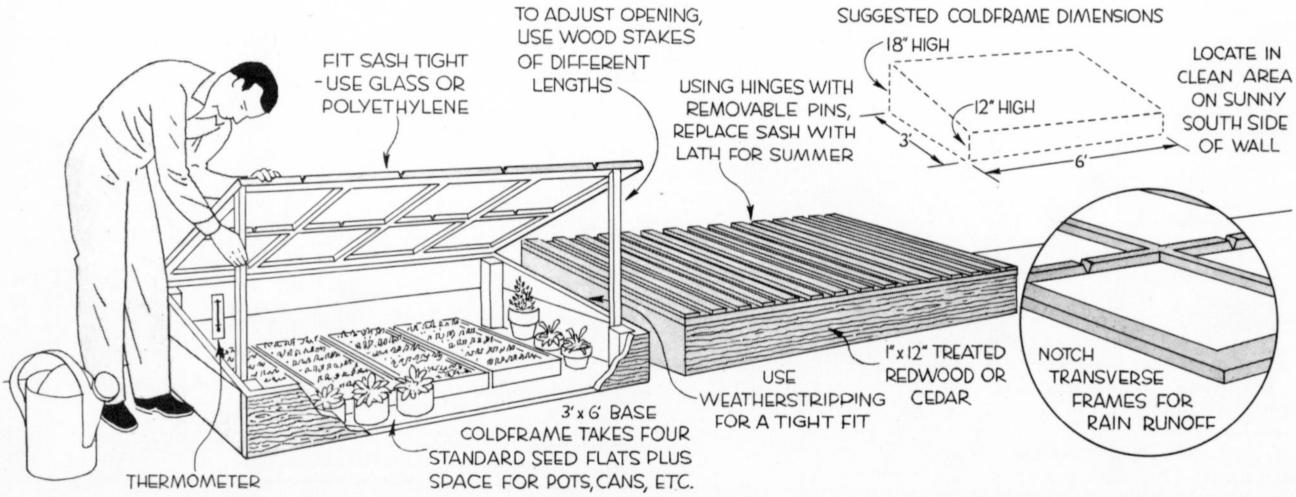

FIT SASH TIGHT - USE GLASS OR POLYETHYLENE

TO ADJUST OPENING, USE WOOD STAKES OF DIFFERENT LENGTHS

USING HINGES WITH REMOVABLE PINS, REPLACE SASH WITH LATH FOR SUMMER

SUGGESTED COLDFRAME DIMENSIONS
18" HIGH
12" HIGH
3'
6'
LOCATE IN CLEAN AREA ON SUNNY SOUTH SIDE OF WALL

1"x 12" TREATED REDWOOD OR CEDAR

USE WEATHERSTRIPPING FOR A TIGHT FIT

NOTCH TRANSVERSE FRAMES FOR RAIN RUNOFF

THERMOMETER

3'x 6' BASE COLDFRAME TAKES FOUR STANDARD SEED FLATS PLUS SPACE FOR POTS, CANS, ETC.

NINE PORTABLE COLDFRAMES

For the person who intends to grow only a few plants for the coming season, a small, portable coldframe is usually all that is required for seed propagation. These temporary plant shelters can be placed conveniently on the south side of the house, near a hose connection, and out of the wind.

You can build a portable coldframe in about an hour, making good use of materials that you may have on hand. Reduced to its simplest form, a coldframe can be nothing more than a box with a transparent roof. Here are some emergency variations for the gardener who needs a coldframe in a hurry.

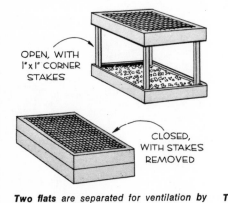

OPEN, WITH 1"x 1" CORNER STAKES

CLOSED, WITH STAKES REMOVED

Two flats *are separated for ventilation by removable corner stakes. Top flat is covered with plastic-wire glass.*

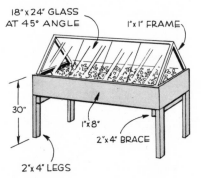

NAIL LATH TO BACK OF FLAT

HEAVY WIRE HELD BY STAPLES

BRICKS

Two supports *are nailed to one end of flat to hold up piece of clear, flexible plastic. Bricks hold plastic in place.*

REMOVE PLYWOOD END NAILED TO 1"x 1" STAKE

TACK PLASTIC TO 1"x 1" STRIP

Stakes *hold plywood ends in place. Ends of stiff wire hoops are pushed into ground to support plastic covering.*

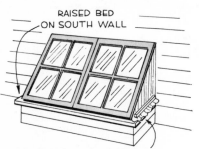

RAISED BED ON SOUTH WALL

COVER ENDS WITH PLASTIC, NAIL TO SASH, WEIGH DOWN BY 1"x 1"

Hinged sash *is attached to side of house for covering raised bed or plant box. Prop cover open for ventilation.*

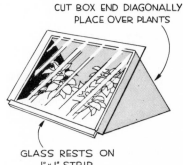

18"x 24" GLASS AT 45° ANGLE

1"x 1" FRAME

30"

1"x 8"

2"x 4" BRACE

2"x 4" LEGS

Elevated plant box *can have glass roof or lath or cheesecloth cover. Board-up ends or use plastic attached with staples.*

CUT BOX END DIAGONALLY PLACE OVER PLANTS

GLASS RESTS ON 1"x 1" STRIP

Wooden box *has bottom, one side removed. Ends are cut at angle to hold glass at a slant to face the sun.*

PIPE OR LUMBER FRAME

2"x 4" ON THICK PLASTIC

U-frame *of lumber or 1-inch pipe in the ground supports tent of plastic. Edges are weighted with bricks or battens.*

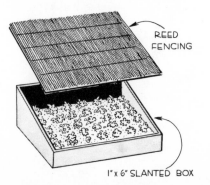

REED FENCING

1"x 6" SLANTED BOX

Slanted box *of 1-inch boards has light-weight cover of reed fencing attached to battens to give filtered sunlight.*

WIRE COAT HANGERS

TUCK PLASTIC UNDER FLAT

Wire coat hangers *are hung on dowel supported by two wood posts, giving a tent frame for the plastic cover.*

Substantial shade structures for plants

As soon as the weather turns warm, most gardens require some sort of shade structure to protect young and tender plants. You may feel that all you need for one or two summers is a portable shade device such as the ones shown on the opposite page—something that can be dismantled or put away until needed again. Actually, there is no reason why a shade structure can-

not become a permanent part of your garden, provided it is well designed and soundly built. Below are four structures that are easy to build. All give light and airy shade. The ones of wood construction should be stained or painted before final installation. The one with aluminum tubing can be left to weather naturally.

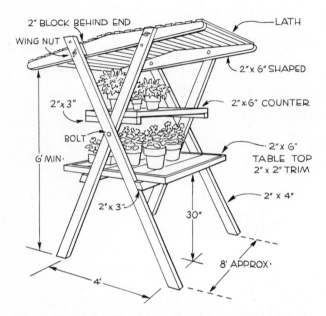

Scissor frame has adjustable overhead to protect shade loving plants on a warm terrace. Lath overhead of 1 by 2-inch wood strips is covered by reed or split bamboo to cut afternoon sun, breeze. Paint frame bright color to contrast with reed color.

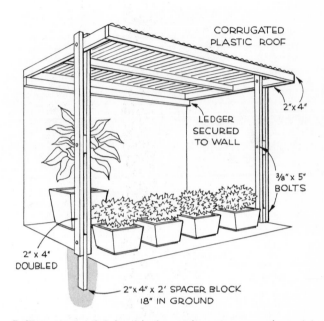

Built-up posts of 2 by 4-inch members are spaced apart to receive the overhead rafters and the wood pin that goes into the ground. The overhead shade may be lightweight corrugated asbestos board or corrugated plastic.

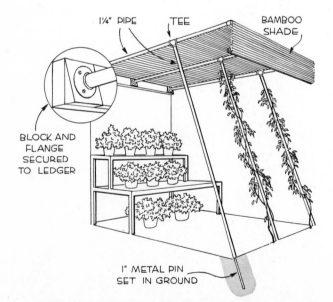

Aluminum pipe frame forms a lightweight support for bamboo shade or reeds along the house wall. Structure is made of pipe, with pipe rafters screwed to house ledger board, and pipe posts secured in ground with metal pins.

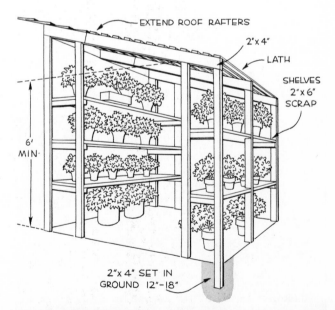

Extension of rafters makes a simple shelter for plants or work space. Rafters should be spaced to match the roof members but should not be more than 32 inches apart. Secure with bolts. Make the shelves 1½ inches thick to give maximum support.

Temporary plant shelters

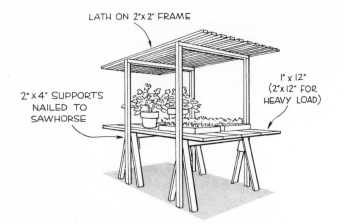

Lath-shaded table is made up of two sawhorses and four 1 by 2-inch or 2 by 12-inch planks 6 feet long. Make the sawhorses higher than is usual—36 inches—for other purposes later on.

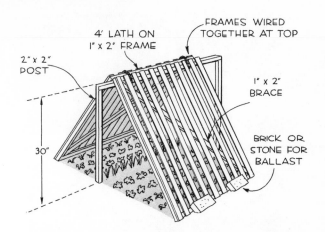

Tent shelter of lath is supported by 2 by 2-inch wood members. The lath shade frames are wired together at the top and have diagonal braces of 1 by 2. Use bricks or stakes to keep in place.

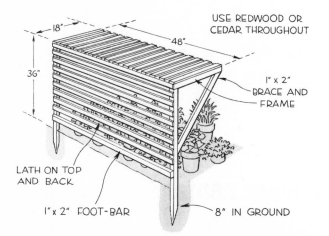

Lightweight sun shade can be moved to accommodate changes in direction of sun as the seasons change. Support posts are easily driven into the ground; brace adds to stability of the roof.

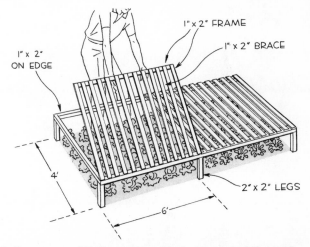

Lath screen and frame moves easily to any part of the garden. Can be used as display rack when plants come into full bloom. To stiffen frame, clinch-nail laths to diagonal brace beneath.

Redwood panels are made of 2 by 2-inch members butted together and secured with galvanized nails (to prevent stains). Each panel corner is braced with triangular pieces of 2 by 4.

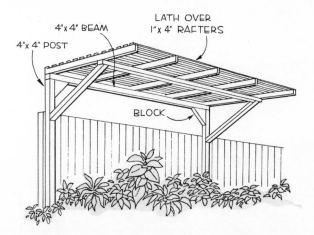

Attached to fence, lath overhang is good device to use when planting shade trees and shade plants. A diagonal 2 by 3-inch brace helps to support the beam. The slats are ½ by 1½-inch.

Double purpose lath work center

This lath lean-to not only provides a potting bench and storage space for garden supplies, it also protects begonias against a hot and dry climate.

The bench unit on the right side is a simply constructed series of shelves. If you like to mix your potting soil on such a work bench, substitute two-inch lumber for the one-inch stock. The pot shelves on the left side could serve equally well as a free-standing garden partition.

The lath roof is made of 1 by 2 redwood, nailed directly to the rafters.

Design: Douglas Baylis.

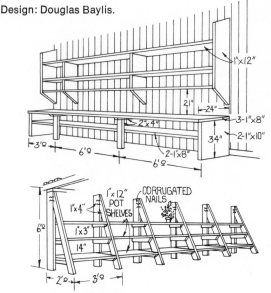

Concealed garden work center

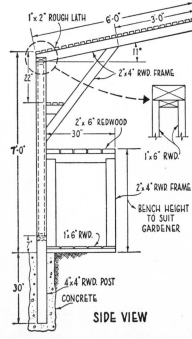

SIDE VIEW

The potting bench shown in the photo at left was designed to fit behind a seven-foot screening fence. There it can easily be shielded from the house or the display areas of a garden.

The overhead shelter is lath. During the winter it can be covered with plastic sheeting, corrugated plastic, or canvas to further protect against frost at night. One section of the lath frame could be made into a solid roof to act as a partial rain shelter.

Design: Osmundson-Staley.

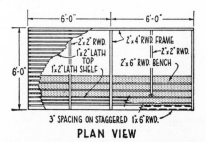

3" SPACING ON STAGGERED 1"x 6" RWD.

PLAN VIEW

Four compact garden work centers

Here are four ways to save space in building a garden work center. Each structure provides just enough space for a potting bench and storage area.

For constructing the framework, redwood and cedar are the most popular materials because of their resistance to decay. In the Northwest, treated fir is commonly used.

Lath makes good overhead protection. For straight lines with no sag, don't use anything smaller than 1 by 2 material. For a more rustic look, use grapestakes or split cedar lath. If you want a solid roof, you can use asphalt roofing paper over a lath framework. Or you can make a more permanent roof with plywood, hardboard, or asbestos board. For a protecting roof that also admits light, use sheet plastic, corrugated plastic, or even glass.

Work surfaces should be reasonably weatherproof, sturdy, and easy to clean. Spaced 2 by 2's or 2 by 3's, about ¼ inch apart, make a strong work top. A solid bench surface of exterior plywood or tempered hardboard is also worth considering. Galvanized or aluminum sheet metal will provide a smooth surface that is easy to care for.

Because of the small area, a gravel flooring is usually adequate; however, you may wish to install a more permanent floor of brick or concrete. (See instructions for working with brick or concrete on pages 48 and 52.)

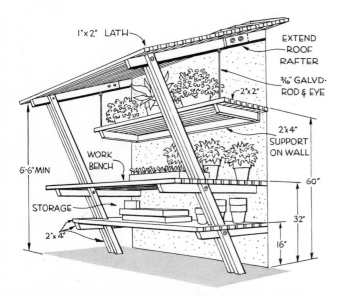

Attached to house rafters, *lath overhead could be covered with sheet plastic. Uprights support overhead, shelf and workbench.*

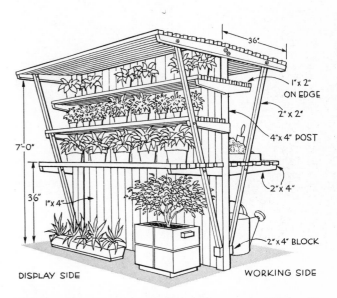

Freestanding work center *is also used as a decorative screen and display area. Face the display side toward living areas.*

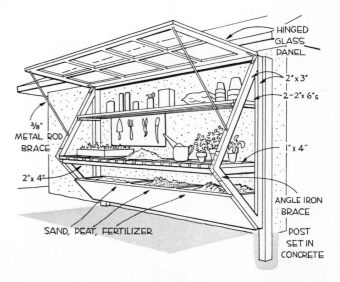

Attached to fence, *workbench has lath top which hinges down to protect plants. Shelf below holds pots, seed flats, soil mix.*

Attached to garage, *by 1-inch strap iron brace, workbench has hinged overhead with glass panels, bins for storage below.*

Storage shed for garden equipment

This combination storage shed and arbor is a simple A-frame construction. It's a place to store all your garden tools, and also such large equipment as power mower, cultivator, and wheelbarrow. Shelves along one side are for storing pots and flats or can be used as a work counter. There is even a loft for storing the usual conglomeration of items no one ever seems to have enough space for.

If storage isn't a need, you could use the structure as a summer house with a shady arbor for outdoor entertaining, as a playhouse for the children, or even as a small weekend house. With little extra work and expense you could fasten canvas on the sides of the arbor to roll down and enclose extra summer sleeping space.

Design: Frank Shell and Dr. Rogers Smith.

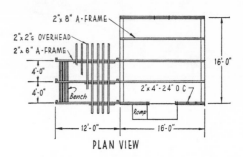

PLAN VIEW

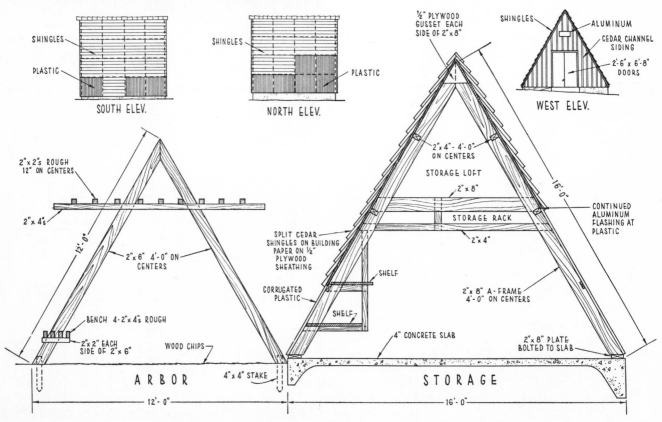

SOUTH ELEV.

NORTH ELEV.

WEST ELEV.

ARBOR

STORAGE

Small windows on front and back of shed open for ventilation, but are not the only sources of light. Plastic panels in the sides admit diffused light. Grape vine covers the arbor at left, creating a cool retreat for warm summer days.

Garden storage in a fence

What looks like a jog in this fence is really a multi-purpose garden storage shed, with a translucent top that lets in light. Each storage area has double doors. One side has shelves, and holds long-handled tools; the other stores large sacks, hoses, a wheeled cart.

The shed blends with the fence because both have a similar facing of 1 by 1-inch cedar strips. The 2 by 6-inch cap holds a sheet of 3/32-inch translucent plastic, slanted to one uncapped end so water will run off (see sketch).

Design: Robert Chittock.

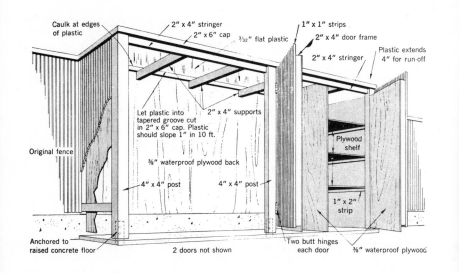

Caulk at edges of plastic
2" x 4" stringer
2" x 6" cap
3/32" flat plastic
1" x 1" strips
2" x 4" door frame
2" x 4" stringer
Plastic extends 4" for run-off
Let plastic into tapered groove cut in 2" x 6" cap. Plastic should slope 1" in 10 ft.
2" x 4" supports
Original fence
Plywood shelf
⅜" waterproof plywood back
4" x 4" post
4" x 4" post
1" x 2" strip
Anchored to raised concrete floor
2 doors not shown
Two butt hinges each door
⅜" waterproof plywood

Storage wall under roof overhang

If you have a wide roof overhang that shields part of a paved side yard, you have a good start toward constructing a convenient storage cabinet.

Construction of the structure shown here, is simple. The cabinet has a 2 by 4-inch frame bolted to a concrete floor. It is sheathed with fixed panels and hinged doors made of 1-inch redwood planks. A roof of ¾-inch plywood supplies necessary bracing.

If you don't have a roof overhang, you could weatherproof a similar cabinet with roll roofing. If you don't want the cabinet next to the house, it could be free standing and function as a screen, or it could use a fence as one wall.

Design: John A. Eliot.

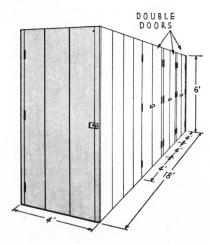

DOUBLE DOORS
6'
4'
18'
4'

Exterior walls of storage cabinet are finished with a clear spar-type varnish. Ordinary hasps serve as handles; have padlocks.

How to avoid drainage problems

Whenever anyone builds a house or garden structure on a piece of ground, the ability of that piece of ground to absorb and gently drain away a downpour of rain is greatly reduced. Roofs and patios do not retain water; they run it off somewhere immediately. And the excavations, fills, and leveling made during any construction change the ground's contours, with the result that puddles and washouts may occur even in a gentle rain.

Most of these drainage problems are usually solved during the actual construction process by some of the means described below, but during the first year that the structure is new, you should keep a close watch on how and where rainwater collects and drains away.

If your house is several years old and your garden is fairly well established, the drainage has probably been well taken care of. It is further helped by landscaping. Established plants and lawns hold soil and water in place, and they transpire a sizable amount of excess rainwater into the atmosphere. But even a fully landscaped home can have some drainage problems that will never go away with the usual procedures. The examples below show you ways in which you can solve them.

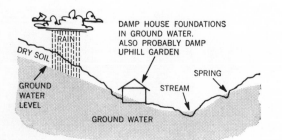

Ground water (rain water which seeps down through the ground). Level is usually deeper below surface on high ground; closer in the valleys. Its nature determines the proper solution.

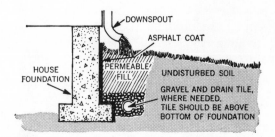

Foundation drainage. Use non-perforated 3 or 4-inch drain pipe to carry the downspout water toward a storm sewer, drainage ditch, or any area that has soft and permeable soil.

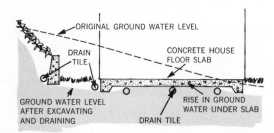

Ground water under slab. Place one or more lines of drain piping underneath the slab before it is laid; completely around perimeter of slab and about a foot below it if already in place.

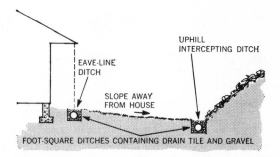

Intercepting ditches. On a sloping lot, use a line of perforated pipe or drainage tile in a foot-wide ditch filled with gravel to carry the water away. Place one ditch under roof line of house.

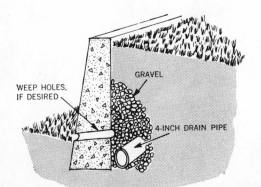

Retaining wall. On hillside lots, use a line of drain pipe or tile laid in a gravel-filled ditch behind the wall to prevent excessive water pressure from building up behind the wall.

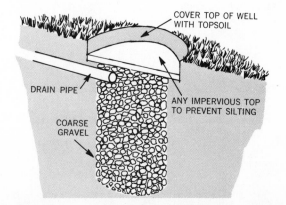

Dry wells. For lowland drainage, dig holes to sandy or gravelly subsoil. (For holes over six feet deep, use a power auger.) Fill holes with coarse gravel, run drain pipe to them, cap with wood.

If you must grade around a big tree

Big trees on your property must have protection when you change the soil level around them. Grading for landscaping or building can cause serious trouble whether you have to remove soil from a tree's root area, or add soil to it. The photographs below show five ways to minimize problems that may occur when either approach is used.

If grading removes only a few inches of soil, you can offset this by applying a thick mulch of peat moss, ground bark, or other organic matter. After a more drastic lowering of grades, it's best to leave the ground close to the tree undisturbed and build a retaining wall, preferably at the drip line under the outermost branches (see photo below on the left).

Raising the grade almost always causes problems. Old trees have lived for years with a certain balance of air, water, and nutrients, and it's hard for them to adjust to sudden changes. Even a few inches of soil piled on top of the root zone seals off enough oxygen to harm roots of trees. Tree walls like the one shown below on the right can reduce the disturbance to the tree's environment. The tree grows in soil at the original level, while farther out the grade is raised.

Cedar wall *retains soil at original level around base of tree next to lowered drive.*

Edging and deck *surround the tree base; area beyond was lowered considerably.*

Stones fill the well *left open in a raised terrace, which lets in air and moisture.*

Bench masks *the open trench around the root crown of this large tree. Galvanized nails join the 2 by 4's for the bench top. The spokes are supported on 4 by 4 posts.*

Redwood edging, *raised platform lets air circulate below in a well 3½ feet deep.*

How to build raised beds

The raised bed is one feature in the garden that justifies the expense and time required to build it. Well designed, it has a strong architectural value. It also introduces into the garden interesting color and texture in wood, stone, brick, adobe, or other materials. When you plan wisely, a raised bed displays plants impressively, and makes a smooth transition from one garden level to another. Here is a discussion of the various ways raised beds can be used in the garden. The sketches below show four ways you can construct raised beds using masonry, lumber, or rustic wood.

TO BRING PLANTS UP CLOSE

A raised bed is perfect for miniature or dwarf plants which are often lost in the garden among taller growing shrubs. If they are brought closer to eye level, you can really enjoy their diminutive charm.

TO MAKE GARDENING EASIER

Gardeners who don't like to do a lot of stooping or bending will find the raised bed a real back saver. Built-up beds are also easier to weed, cultivate, and water. Vegetables tend to produce earlier because a raised bed quickly absorbs the sun's heat.

If you're interested in hybridizing, plant your specialties in raised beds. To help you identify plants, attach a card with the information to the sides of the bed. The plants, besides being close at hand for periodic inspection, are protected from pets and children.

AS A TRANSITION FROM ONE GARDEN LEVEL TO ANOTHER

A raised bed is one of the most successful ways to create a three-dimensional effect or to effect a transition from one level to another.

A gaily planted bed is a perfect buffer between two different garden areas. With a raised bed, you can separate a terrace and parking strip, or a lawn and vegetable garden. In a garden which is perfectly level, you can easily use a raised bed to relieve the monotony of flat surfaces.

FOR PLANTS THAT NEED EXCELLENT DRAINAGE

In gardens with heavy, poorly drained soil, the raised bed makes it possible to grow daphne, gardenias, citrus, and other plants which are sensitive to water-logged soil. Herbs, succulents, cacti, and many Californian and Australian native plants thrive in the warm soil they have in a sunny raised bed.

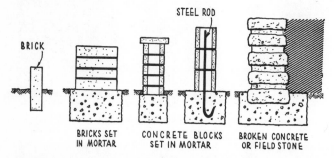

Masonry makes a strong, enduring wall if the footings go down far enough and are heavy enough, as shown here. To relieve water pressure, provide small holes for drainage through wall.

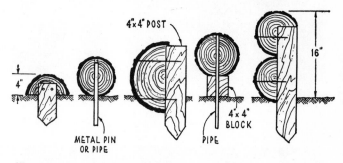

Weathered logs are appropriate for beds with azaleas, fuchsias, or begonias. To get the logs, you may have to go directly to the woods with a truck or trailer and pick them up yourself.

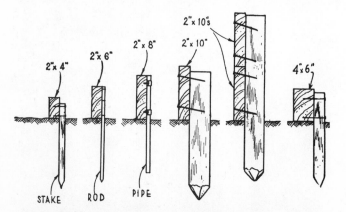

Rough-finished redwood or cedar makes a good-looking low retaining wall. It is easy to install, inexpensive, and weathers well. For longer life treat the stakes with a wood preservative.

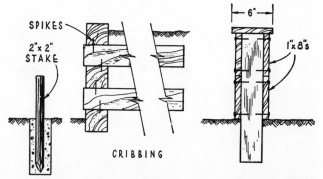

Row of stakes (2 by 2-inch) can be driven directly into the ground, or embedded in a narrow trench filled with concrete. Where the wall supports earth, some cribbing adds strength.

Lengths of redwood 10 and 12 inches high and of varying widths are alternately nailed together; set 10 inches deep in concrete.

Corrugated asbestos sheet is nailed to 4 x 4 redwood posts sunk in ground. Top is rough 2 x 6. Design: William Kapranos.

Hollow concrete blocks are mortared to cast concrete footing and are capped for a finished top. Design: Geraldine Knight.

Railroad ties are nailed together with 12-inch spikes and are then toe-nailed at the joints. Design: Eckbo, Dean & Williams.

Redwood stakes are sunk in ground edge to edge. Can be toe-nailed together at the back. Design: Eckbo, Royston & Williams.

Rough redwood boards are nailed together in zig-zag pattern. 2 by 6 cap mitered at ends. Design: Thomas Church & Assoc.

More ways to use raised beds

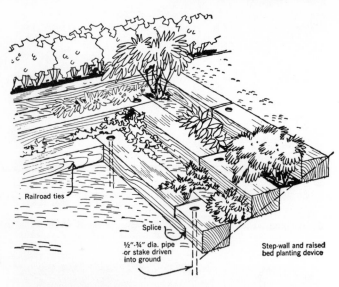

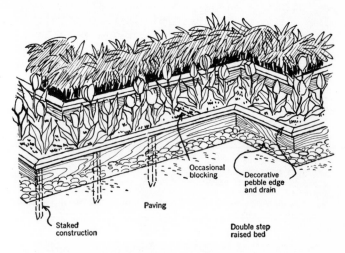

THREE-STEP BED OF RAILROAD TIES

If you have a problem of change in level in the garden, consider the practicality and attractiveness of the one, two, or three-step raised bed. Although the sketch above shows a raised bed with the railroad ties turning a corner, they could just as easily be extended 40 to 60 feet across a slope and serve as a substitute for a retaining wall. The same idea could be carried out with concrete blocks set in sand or mortar or with 2 by 10-inch redwood planks set vertically.

Design: Douglas Baylis.

TWO-STEP RAISED BED FOR GRADUAL SLOPE

A two-level raised bed is suitable for a modest change of level — perhaps 12 to 20 inches — between upper and lower garden areas. Planted with colorful plants, or shrubs, a double raised bed is more decorative and pleasant to live with than many other types of low retaining walls. If you have a gradual slope from the rear of the house up to the property line, a series of such double-step raised beds can be built to create a number of usable level terraces.

Design: Douglas Baylis.

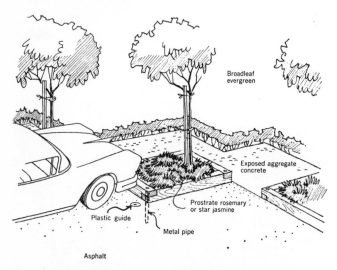

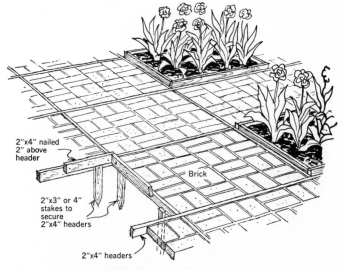

A RAISED BED TO REGULATE GUEST PARKING

In a tight guest-parking area, a series of car-wide raised beds can help you make the most of available parking space. Such beds can also serve as tree islands. Edgings or painted lines on the paving will help guide arriving cars into parking spots. Or you can insert reflector buttons at intervals in the paving. If the area is not marked, careless parking might put 2 cars in a 3-car space or 3 cars in a 4-car space; but most drivers obey guide lines and do not park across them.

RAISED BEDS WITHIN TERRACE PAVING

Terrace paving is often laid out in an arrangement of squares or rectangles set off by edgings. Such paving can be much more pleasant if occasional rectangles are left open as planting beds. And these planting beds will work better if the terrace is laid on sub-soil. If your paving edgings are 2 by 4's, all you have to do is nail an additional 2 by 4 liner 2 inches higher than the edging. Almost 6 inches of top-soil is then above the adjacent sub-soil level providing excellent drainage.

Wood edgings for patios, walkways, paths

Wood edgings (often called header boards) not only make neat demarcations between lawns, flower beds, and other planting areas, but they also make handsome edging and division strips for brick, concrete, or other garden paving. Here are some suggestions to consider when installing wood edgings:

Use heart redwood or cedar — both are highly resistant to rot. Painting the lumber with a wood preservative before installation will prolong its life; if there are termites in the area, a preservative containing a termite poison may be a good precaution.

To prevent lumber from splitting (particularly stakes), use galvanized box nails (similar to common nails, but thinner).

The most popular edgings are made of 2 by 4-inch lumber, either rough-cut (2 inches thick) or finished (1½ inches thick). You can also use 3 by 4 or 4 by 4 lumber for heavier edgings, if no bending for curves is required.

Use stakes of 1 by 2's, 2 by 2's, or 1 by 4's, 12 inches long, and locate them no more than 5 feet apart. Also place one

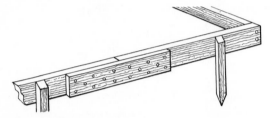

stake close to each corner and on each side of a splice. (Splices can be 1 by 4's or 2 by 4's, about 2 feet long, see sketch above.) If your edging simply divides two cultivated areas, you can alternate the stakes on opposite sides of the

edging. If it borders a lawn, place all stakes on the sides away from the grass so that you will be able to run a lawn edger along the edging without interference.

To form a curved edging, nail thin, more flexible boards together, staggering the splices, until the laminated board is the thickness desired around the curve. Many lumberyards stock "resawn" boards (½ and 1 inch thick) for curved edgings.

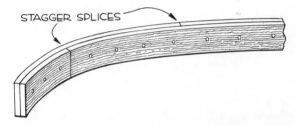

The ½-inch resawn boards are usually far from uniform in thickness — they vary from 5/16 to 5/8 inch. The trick is to measure the approximate radius of the curve you wish to form, then go to a lumberyard and try bending different ½-inch thicknesses to find which will make the best curve.

STEP-BY-STEP INSTALLATION OF EDGINGS

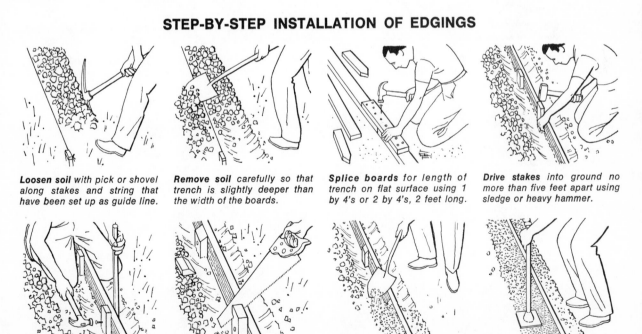

Loosen soil with pick or shovel along stakes and string that have been set up as guide line.

Remove soil carefully so that trench is slightly deeper than the width of the boards.

Splice boards for length of trench on flat surface using 1 by 4's or 2 by 4's, 2 feet long.

Drive stakes into ground no more than five feet apart using sledge or heavy hammer.

Drive nails into stake and edging using back-up block of sledge, crowbar lever, rock.

Cut tops of stakes on bevel with a handsaw; top of bevel should be as high as edging.

Replace soil on outside of edging so that it is flush with the top surface of the wood.

Use tamper to pack the soil tightly against the edging and stakes. Leave stakes in place.

A variety of paving choices

The fifteen photographs on these two pages give an idea of the wide variety of paving choices available to the homeowner. The following pages discuss six of the most popular surfacing materials, describe their advantages and their shortcomings, and give specific construction pointers.

No one type of paving will meet an individual's specifications 100 per cent. Here are some points that you will want to take into consideration before making a final decision:

1. Surface Texture: Does it provide a pleasant feeling underfoot or is it too rough? Is it soft enough for young children to play on, yet solid enough for fast-moving games? What type of drainage will be required?

2. Appearance: Will the color, pattern, or texture blend in with the other surroundings and other surfaces?

3. Durability: What will weather do to it? How much of your time will be required to keep it looking nice? Do you want temporary paving or one that is long-lasting?

4. Cost: Are the materials expensive or moderately priced? Can you save on costs by doing the job yourself? Are there any hidden costs such as changes in natural drainage or increased property tax valuation?

5. Application: If you want to do the job yourself, is the paving a material you can handle? Do you have to transport the materials yourself? How long will it take you to do the job? What weather conditions are the most suitable for installation?

6. Maintenance: How easy will the paving be to clean? Does it require constant raking, sweeping, or hosing? Will weeds grow through it?

Gravel of varied colors, separated by redwood edgings, makes decorative shapes.

Beach pebbles arranged in the bottom of a shallow pool simulate a natural pond.

Redwood rounds set in 2-in. gravel leads to entry; area sprayed with weed killer.

Crushed rock path is separated from the loose coarse-gravel bed by wood edging.

Broken tile set in concrete in fan-shaped pattern gives a rich color and texture.

Flat, smooth stones pressed into mortar separate the stone-like concrete sections.

Wood blocks are made from sections of old heavy timbers, set with end-grain up.

Concrete blocks are given a light broom-brushed surface; Irish moss in between.

Buff bricks keep enclosed patio bright. Jack-on-jack pattern needed no cutting.

Simulated block paving created by filling scored lines in wet concrete with mortar.

Crushed rock pressed into tinted concrete blocks gives paving sparkled effect.

Large pebbles are seeded in concrete strip running between two smooth areas.

Flagstones are set on hard ground; the joints are planted with creeping thyme.

Brick edging separates asphalt driveway from built-up flower bed and garden area.

Exposed aggregate, edged with cobbled paving wide enough for a garden bench.

Paving with bricks

The basic form, composition, and fabrication of brick have undergone little change over 5,000 years. Heavy clay and soil and water are mixed, molded, or cut into blocks, and then baked in a kiln. Properly fired brick is hard enough to last for centuries and shows only minor wear.

There are two basic kinds of bricks: common and face. Most garden paving is done with common bricks. People like their familiar color and texture, and also their lower price. Face bricks (more uniform in size and color) are not as widely available as common, and only recently have they been used to any degree in garden paving.

The exact dimensions of a standard brick (both common and face) vary from region to region and manufacturer to manufacturer. In the West, standard dimensions are about 2½ by 3¾ by 8 inches.

Brick looks well almost anywhere you want to put it, but there are two important considerations before you start paving: (1) Water must drain away from the area you pave, since shifting and efflorescence (see detailed explanation below under the discussion of cleaning mortar off bricks) can result if water is allowed to stand under brick paving. (2) In choosing a bond or pattern for your bricks, consider the degree of potential difficulty in laying that pattern. Some bonds demand a good bit of accuracy and brick cutting; others are relatively simple.

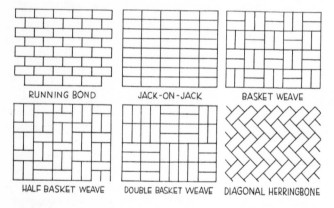

RUNNING BOND   JACK-ON-JACK   BASKET WEAVE

HALF BASKET WEAVE   DOUBLE BASKET WEAVE   DIAGONAL HERRINGBONE

PREPARING THE BASE

Start by setting up wood edgings (a framework usually made of 1 by 4's or 2 by 4's) around the entire area you intend to pave. Once this area is framed, divide it with a temporary edging into a smaller section (the sections can run the length of the area). After you pave a small section, move the edging over. For example, an area 20 feet by 20 feet can be divided every 5 feet with temporary edgings to make sections 20 feet long and 5 feet wide. Once you begin to set the bricks, it's easier to keep them even in a small area.

When edgings are in place, turn over the soil and pulverize it, then screed it smooth. So that you will have adequate drainage, grade the area to slope at least 1 inch every 6 feet, then tamp or roll it until the surface is hard and flat.

HOW TO SET BRICKS ON SAND

Setting bricks on sand is the easiest method for the beginner. After compacting the soil, spread sand to a depth of 1 to 2

inches between the edgings. Wet the sand moderately to help it settle. Using a screed (a 2 by 4 that rides on the edgings with an extension that reaches down to the level of the sand), level the sand for about 3 feet between the edgings. Lay the bricks on the sand (being careful not to disturb it so that it becomes uneven) in the pattern you have chosen, so that they butt up tightly against one another. Tap any high brick into the sand with a rubber mallet or a hammer handle. Use a spirit level often to make sure the bricks are on the level you want. Then screed the next 3 feet, and repeat the process until all the bricks are in place.

Throw handfuls of fine sand out across the bricks and let it dry completely in the sun for a few hours. Then sweep it into the cracks. Using a hose nozzle that gives a fine spray, wet the area to settle the sand between the cracks.

HOW TO SET BRICKS OVER CONCRETE

It's an easy matter to pave over a concrete path or patio with brick. First set up edgings around the concrete. Then spread ½ inch of mortar (3 parts plastering sand, 1 part cement, ⅓ part fire clay or lime) over an area of about 3 feet, and screed it. Have the bricks moistened slightly before setting them. Set the bricks firmly in place, butting them up against each other and leveling them, but don't tap them down. Let them set for about 24 hours, then sweep fine sand into the cracks.

HOW TO SET BRICKS ON DRY MORTAR

Brick on dry mortar is not as stable as brick on concrete, but it will make a good solid surface where the subsoil is sound, and where heavy freezing is not a problem. The mortar keeps weeds from coming up between the brick and also keeps water from draining down through.

Start by spreading the area with a 2-inch base of sand. Then place the bricks on the sand, leaving at least a ¼-inch opening between each one. The dry mixture to go between the bricks is made of 1 part cement and 4 parts sand. Throw it out across the bricks and then sweep it into the cracks. Make sure that the bricks are dry when you throw on the mix or it will stick to the tops. Use a hand brush to push the dry mortar between the bricks, then a broom to sweep away the excess. Sprinkle the area with a fine spray.

Let the mortar set for about 2 hours, then use a wet burlap sack to scrub the top of each brick as clean as you can get it. After the paving is completely dry, go over it with mortar cleaner as described on the opposite page.

HOW TO SET BRICKS IN WET MORTAR

Setting bricks in wet mortar is the best procedure if you want a clean, tooled, or shaped mortar joint between the bricks and if you want a more durable paving where winters are severe. The bricks can be laid on any properly prepared base, including existing concrete.

First wet the bricks, otherwise they will suck the water out of the wet mortar mix and it won't bind. A good procedure is to spray them with a hose in the morning for setting in the afternoon.

Lay the damp bricks in a ½-inch mortar base leaving a ½-inch joint between them, and let them set for about 4 hours. For the mortar between the joints, use 4 parts plastering sand, 1 part cement, but no fire clay as is used for setting bricks over concrete. (Fire clay helps make the mixture stick and this quality is not needed here.) Using a flat, pointed trowel, push the mortar into the joints, and let it set about ½ hour or until the joints are thumbprint hard. Then point the joints with the edge of a steel rod, pipe, or other rounded tool.

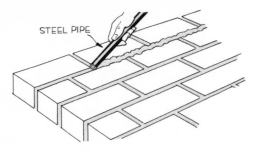

STEEL PIPE

HOW TO CLEAN MORTAR OFF BRICKS

Caring for brick once it's in is not a big job, but it is important if you want to keep your paving handsome.

Cleaning up spilled mortar while you are working is the first safeguard. Try to work as cleanly as possible; if you drop excess mortar on the bricks, you can save time and effort by wiping it up immediately with a wet piece of burlap.

To remove mortar that has dried on brick, use a solution of 1 part muriatic acid to 9 parts water. Begin by soaking the area to be cleaned with a fine spray of water to saturate it and cut down the capillary action of the bricks. Let the water settle in, then brush the area with the acid solution (wear gloves and use a plastic bucket). Rinse thoroughly with a hose to prevent acid stains from remaining on the bricks.

The white deposit that sometimes appears on brick paving after it's wetted by rain or hosing is called efflorescence and is caused by water-soluble salts in the bricks or in the setting bed rising to the surface through capillary action. When the water dries, the salts crystallize into a white crust. In most cases where common brick has been used, it will be a matter of years before the salts have all come to the surface and efflorescence ceases. Efflorescence is not harmful, but it can be unsightly.

Muriatic acid or a stiff brush will remove the dried salts. Brush them loose and sweep them away. Don't try to hose them off, as the water will only drive them back down into the bricks and the process will begin all over again the next time the bricks get wet.

HOW TO LAY BRICKS IN DRY MORTAR

Almost everyone who has tackled the job of laying bricks has some opinions on ways to make the job easier. If you are a beginning bricklayer, it is a good idea to talk to friends and neighbors who have worked with brick and who may have some helpful suggestions. Don't be in too big a hurry to start laying the brick.

Take time to experiment with various patterns and grid sizes before you begin. As a helpful guide, the six sketches below offer a step-by-step procedure for laying bricks in dry mortar. Most of the operations also apply to laying bricks over existing concrete, in sand, and in wet mortar.

Spread sand between edgings to a depth of 1 to 2 inches. Then wet the sand with a fine spray to help it settle.

Screed sand about 3 feet at a time. Once bricks are in place, screed next 3 feet; set bricks even with those already laid.

Work forward from bricks already laid. Here bricks laid running bond are tamped into place with the handle of a mallet.

Cut bricks for fit by setting brick on sand, holding wide chisel in place, and using heavy mallet to give chisel a firm tap.

Use hand brush to sweep dry mortar into ½-inch separation between bricks; sweep away excess with hand or push broom.

Use fine spray to wet area, being careful not to wash mortar out of joints. Let mortar set 2 hours before scrubbing bricks clean.

Paving with flagstone

A flagstone pavement not only is durable and solid, but if properly constructed, it can last forever. For many people this lasting quality far outweighs the fact that flagstone is a relatively expensive paving material.

There are many different types and colors of flagstone to choose from. The colors are subdued—yellow, brownish red, gray, buff—any of which adds a mellow warmth to the garden floor. The shape is either irregular or rectangular, the latter costing more because of the expense involved in cutting. Some types of flagstone can easily be cut on the job, with a wide chisel as shown in the sketch below or simply by breaking over

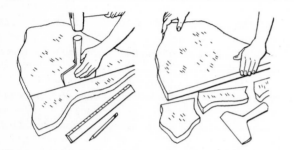

the edge of a 2 by 4 (the latter is more risky because it often doesn't produce a straight cut). Thicknesses vary from ½ inch to 3 inches. A 2-inch thickness is required if you want to pave over a sand bed; a 1-inch thickness is ample for paving over a concrete slab.

SETTING FLAGSTONES IN SOIL

One of the easiest ways to lay thick flagstone paving is to place the stone directly on the soil. If the area to be paved has good drainage and is not too large, this method is quite satisfactory. The stones may shift and settle slightly during wet weather, but they still provide a good footing.

A more permanent method for setting flagstones in soil is to first remove the soil to a depth of slightly less than the thickness of the stones. Then fit the stones in place, adjusting the soil to fit the underneath contours of each piece.

SETTING FLAGSTONES IN SAND

The method for laying flagstones in sand is essentially the same as used for bricks but has two main differences: (1) After the bed of sand has been laid and thoroughly screeded, set the stones in place, working them down until they are well imbedded. (2) Lay all the stones before filling in the joints, so that you can study the effect of the pattern and make adjustments accordingly.

Once you have achieved the pattern you desire, fill in the joints with soil. Do this carefully so that the soil is not flush with the surface of the stones. Then wet the area thoroughly with a fine spray.

SETTING FLAGS ON CONCRETE

This method requires that the flagstones be bedded in a layer of mortar spread over a permanent base of concrete at least 3 inches thick. It also requires that you try out your pattern as described above *before* setting the stones permanently in place.

Use a wet but not soupy mix of 1 part cement to 3 parts sand and spread it on the concrete base in small areas, covering just enough to place one or two stones. Then while the mortar bed is still damp, lay the stones in place and firmly tamp them down using a trowel handle. Use a straightedge to check for level.

Allow the stones to set for at least 24 hours. Then fill in the joints with grout (a mixture of 1 part cement, 3 parts sand, and ⅓ part lime or fireclay) and smooth the surface with a pointed trowel. Before the grout dries, wipe off any excess mortar with a clean, damp cloth.

CASTING CONCRETE FLAGSTONES

You can obtain pleasing results by casting imitation flagstone paving in concrete. Not only is this method less expensive than buying real flags, but it allows you to produce the exact effect that you desire in color, pattern, and texture.

To cover a large area with cast concrete flagstones you will need to build a wooden grid form that will make several stones at one filling (see page 53 for an easy-to-make form). The inner surfaces should be smooth and slightly flared out toward the bottom for easy removal after the concrete sets up slightly.

Before you begin, thoroughly soak the form with water. Greasing or oiling the inside of the form with soap or engine oil will help prevent the cement from adhering to the wood. Put the form down on soil that has been graded and tamped level and fill each compartment with concrete. After it has set slightly, remove the framework, smooth the edges of the blocks, and set up again for the next section of paving. Let the castings set for 24 hours before moving them and handle them gently for three weeks.

You can also cast individual concrete flagstones for stepping stones in a simple wooden form or in a dirt mold right where they are going to be laid. Make a form with 2 by 4's, nailing two corners together, hinging the second and third, and putting a hook on the fourth (see sketch below). Place the form over building paper, oil it, and pour in concrete that has been mixed 1 part cement, 2 parts sand, and 3 parts gravel. When the concrete has set up slightly, remove the form and smooth off any rough edges with a trowel. Clean the form, re-oil, and refill with concrete. Keep the completed blocks damp for three days.

The easiest method for making stepping stones is to pour concrete right in depressions in the ground where you want them. Remove the soil for each stepping stone to a depth of 4 inches and fill with the same concrete mixture as described above. Use a wood float to trowel the surface smooth, and keep it damp for 3 days. If the stones are cast in a lawn, the surface of the stones should be slightly below the lawn so a mower can easily pass over them.

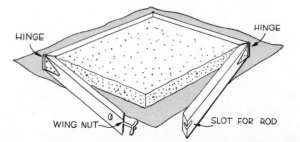

HINGE

HINGE

WING NUT

SLOT FOR ROD

Paving with tile

For paving and garden flooring, tile ranks high in durability, color, and stain-resistance, but like flagstone, it is expensive. However, tile has some unique advantages. It is suitable for large or small areas; it cleans and waxes easily; it is especially good around a barbecue, in a potting shed, on a walkway around a swimming pool, on paths, on a deck.

Two types of tile are most suitable underfoot. Patio tile is a brick-red color and comes only in 12-inch squares or 6 by 12-inch half-sizes. Quarry tile is more expensive, but comes in smaller square and rectangular sizes, and in several tones from brick red to gray.

Some homeowners would rather have a professional do the setting of tile rather than trust themselves with such a heavy investment in materials. However, the average weekend mason can lay tile if he will work with precision and care.

You can lay tile in sand, over concrete, or over wood (see sketches below). As an outdoor paving material, it is laid most often on a 1-inch mortar bed put directly on the ground. Here is the procedure:

PLAN AHEAD

To eliminate unnecessary tile cutting, plan your area to accommodate the dimensions of the tile-plus-joints. Allow for ¾ inch of mortar between larger tiles, ½ inch for the smaller sizes. If you find that you need to cut only a few tiles, you can chip them to size with a cold chisel. Draw your cutting line with a pencil. Then carefully chip away a little at a time. If you have to cut tiles in quantity, it is better to mark the tiles where they should be cut and take them to a stoneyard, where they can be sawed with a diamond saw.

If your patio or walk calls for a curved edge, cut the tiles in a series of angles that correspond roughly with the curve and fill in the edges or separations with mortar. You can also lay brick in mortar on top of the cut edges to give the appearance of a curved border.

To estimate mortar quantity, allow 1 sack of Portland cement and 4 cubic feet of sand for every 35 square feet of surface. Use this ratio for 12 by 12-inch tile with ¾-inch joints. Smaller tile sizes, with more joints, require slightly more mortar.

SETTING THE TILES IN MORTAR

Begin by soaking your tiles in clean, clear water for at least 15-20 minutes. Level the soil 1 to 1½ inches below the desired grade, and tamp or roll the ground until the depressions are filled in and the soil has settled. Then mix five parts of clean sand with one part of cement until no streaks of gray or brown are showing. Add water and continue mixing until the mortar is smooth but slightly stiff. Spread only enough mix on the ground that can be covered with tile within an hour, as the tile should be laid while the mortar is still plastic, not set. A good procedure is to mix only enough for 20 square feet at first to find out how fast you can work.

Remove several tiles from the water, stand them on edge to drain off surface water, and place them on the mortar bed while they are still damp. Tap each tile with the handle of a hammer until it is firmly bedded, also using a straightedge to make sure you get a smooth, flush surface.

Within 24 hours, you can fill the spaces between the tiles with joining mortar: one part cement and three parts sand, with enough water so that mix will pour easily. Use an old watering pot or a coffee can with the lip bent to pour the mix into the joints. Fill the joints flush and trowel them smooth with a mason's trowel.

Clean up any spills immediately with a wet cloth. It is not necessary to keep tile wet after laying, but don't walk on it for at least three days.

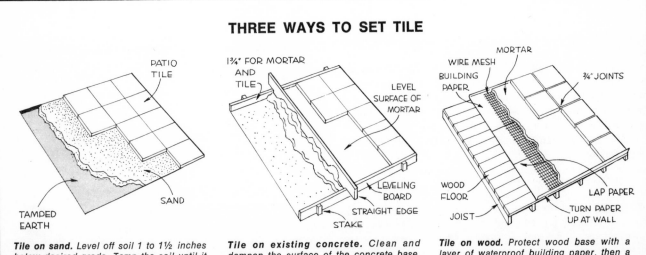

THREE WAYS TO SET TILE

Tile on sand. *Level off soil 1 to 1½ inches below desired grade. Tamp the soil until it is smooth and pour on the sand. Butt the tiles together or leave ½ to ¾-inch joints. Use edgings to keep tile in place.*

Tile on existing concrete. *Clean and dampen the surface of the concrete base. If existing pad is smooth, roughen it with diluted muriatic wash. Rinse and let dry. Spread ¾-inch mortar bed and set tile.*

Tile on wood. *Protect wood base with a layer of waterproof building paper, then a mesh of ¾-inch chicken or stucco wire kept ¼-inch above wood base to reinforce mortar. Apply 1-inch mortar bed.*

Paving with concrete

Concrete is the most versatile of all garden paving materials. It can have a surface plain and smooth enough for dancing or roller skating, or it can have a rough or patterned texture. These extremes are possible because concrete is a plastic material which will take almost any form and which can be finished in a wide variety of surface textures. Despite these advantages, some homemakers make concrete their last choice as a garden paving material. They claim it is hard, has a cold, industrial quality, and is a difficult material to handle.

CONCRETE FORMULA

Since concrete is a mixture of cement, sand, gravel, and water, its character is determined by the proportions used for these four ingredients. The formula recommended for garden paving is 1 part cement, 2¼ parts sand, and 3 parts gravel or crushed rock. Add about 5 gallons of water for each sack of cement used. The water should be clean and pure, the sand must be clean river sand, and the gravel or crushed rock should be 1 inch maximum in size.

HOW TO BUY CONCRETE

It is possible to buy concrete for paving in the garden in any of the three ways listed below. The advantages and disadvantages of each are also listed.

Bulk dry materials. You buy the required amounts of sand, cement, and gravel. Unless you have ample storage space, buy only what you need for the project at hand.

Advantages: Buying the materials dry and in bulk is the cheapest way you can get it. You can mix any amount that is convenient for you to use, whenever you are ready to go to work.

Disadvantages: You must have a place where you can store sand and gravel. The cement sacks must be kept absolutely dry. This generally means covered storage.

Ready mix or transit mix. Concrete in this form is delivered to your home, ready to be poured in place.

Advantages: No mixing equipment is needed. The concrete can be prepared according to any specifications before delivery. You get well-mixed concrete every time.

Disadvantages: An extra charge is usually made for delivery of any quantity under 2 or 3 cubic yards. Some plants will deliver as little as ½-cubic yard under this arrangement, but others will deliver nothing less than one yard. There is an extra charge if the truck has to wait a length of time after it arrives on the site. Delivery can be difficult as the trucks are often too large and too heavy for a driveway.

Dry ready-mix. You can buy sacks of all-purpose concrete suitable for most home uses in 50, 100, and 150-pound sizes — containing the correct proportions of sand, cement, and gravel. You can also buy a sand-gravel mix to combine with cement.

Advantages: There is no guesswork. All you have to do is add water, mix, and the concrete is ready to use. It is ideal for patching old jobs or doing small piecemeal work.

Disadvantages: Dry ready-mix is relatively expensive. The cost is about three to four times that of either bulk dry materials or transit mix. But, if you don't have storage space or don't need large quantities of concrete mix, this is probably the most practical way for you to obtain it.

WORK CAREFULLY TO MAKE GOOD CONCRETE

An important factor in your concrete mix is its ratio of water to cement. Concrete hardens because the powder-like cement and water form an adhesive which locks the sand and pebbles together. Too much water thins or dilutes this adhesive paste and weakens its cementing qualities; too little, and you can't work it.

If you are working with small quantities, you can mix your concrete on a platform or in a wheelbarrow with a shovel or hoe. An existing concrete slab will do, or you can make a platform out of old lumber or scrap plywood. Measure the quantity of sand, spread it out evenly, and spread the cement on top. Turn and mix the dry ingredients until there are no streaks of color. Add gravel or rock and mix until they are evenly distributed through the mixture. Then make a depression in the mixture and slowly add the water, turning the ingredients until they are thoroughly combined. Use a rolling motion with a shovel to save energy and speed the job. For larger quantities, it is best to rent an electric mixer. There are two standard size mixers available. The smaller one holds about two cubic feet of mix and will fit into the trunk of your car with the lid up. The larger machine holds about three cubic feet and is mounted on a trailer which hooks onto your bumper.

SURFACE TEXTURE IS IMPORTANT

If you are doing your own concrete finishing, you can create an unlimited range of textures. Be sure that the finish you choose is the right one for the service it will perform. Here are two popular choices:

Smooth finish. For the smoothest surface, use a steel trowel. Add non-skid texture by brushing the surface with a broom. Experiment with different bristled brooms for a wide variety of finish. For the roughest "smooth" surface, use a wood float — don't finish with the steel trowel.

Exposed aggregate. One of the most time consuming surfaces to handle is exposed aggregate. Some craftsmen do the job with a hose and push broom to remove the top surface of sand and cement. Others use a stiff wire brush and a hose.

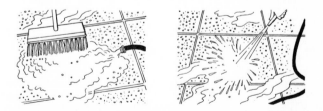

Make sure that the surface is level — a wood float usually works satisfactorily. Then let the concrete set up until you can walk on it. Then gently try brushing and hosing. If the concrete is too soft, wait another hour or two before exposing the aggregate. Scrub the surface with a solution of muriatic acid and water, which removes some more of the cement and sand.

HOW TO CONSTRUCT A CONCRETE PATIO

Remove sod and soil from area to be paved. Use tamper to compact the soil and make it fairly even and smooth.

Secure edgings by driving stakes slightly lower than height of edgings and nailing securely with galvanized nails.

Spread sand evenly to a depth of 2 inches over the area. Dampen the sand using a fine spray to help it settle completely.

Cover dividers that are to be left in place with a layer of masking tape before pouring the concrete. Leave stakes in place.

Pour concrete into one section at a time. Space or rake the concrete well into the corners; overfill the forms slightly.

Use straightedge to strike-off concrete so that it is level with height of forms; but don't try to get a smooth surface.

Trowel concrete using a wooden float, which gives it a rough surface. Use a steel trowel for a denser, smooth surface.

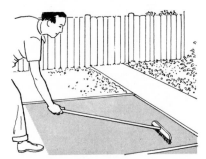

Use broom with fine bristles to produce interesting texture, cut down surface glare, and provide good traction.

Cover with plastic weighted at the edges to seal in moisture of curing. Keep surface covered for at least five days.

Courtesy of Portland Cement Association

HOW TO MAKE PRE-CAST STEPPING STONES

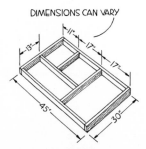

DIMENSIONS CAN VARY

Wood frame is easy to build; has common wire handles on ends. Work concrete mix into form with trowel, then strike off the surface with a wood float, giving it a rough, non-skid texture.

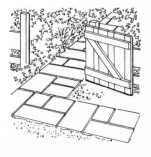

Lift form gently off concrete after it has set up slightly. Use two trowels to edge around each paver; keep concrete damp for several days. Completed walk has a modular pattern.

Pebble paving

One of the most favored paving methods is to press stones into a concrete base. This paving holds up well and is easy to reset should any of the stones become dislodged. There is no limit to the size, color, or texture of the stones you can use. Many building supply yards carry a wide variety of stones to choose from, ranging from the size of peas to double the size of a fist.

Pebble paving provides a texture quite different from that of the usual exposed aggregate finish (see discussion and procedure on page 52); you add the pebbles or smooth rocks after the concrete is poured—something like pressing raisins into a pan of dough. How far you press them determines the smoothness of the finish.

Of all the paving examples shown in this book, pebble paving offers the greatest possibilities in design, since each stone can be hand-placed. You can make swirls, circles, even whimsical forms using stones collected on a vacation trip or carefully selected at the stone yard. Since placement of each stone into a design is time-consuming, you may want to confine pebble paving to a relatively small walk or patio section.

FOR THOSE WHO WANT A COBBLED SURFACE

Probably the easiest approach to pebble paving is to simply press large cobbles or stones into a wet concrete base. Be sure to press or pound them far enough down that the concrete grips the stones. This surface usually is not intended for foot traffic. Let the paving harden for several days and then clean the stones with a 10 per cent solution of muriatic acid to remove excess mortar and to bring out the pebbles' colors.

FOR THOSE WHO WANT A SEEDED SURFACE

With this method, the concrete is laid down as for any walk or patio slab and then selected pebbles are sprinkled over the surface and wood-floated into the soft concrete. Before the concrete sets up, the pebble surfaces are re-exposed by hosing and brushing just as you do with concrete paving to produce an exposed aggregate surface.

The tricky part of this procedure is choosing the exact time of exposing the pebbles while the concrete is hardening.

PEBBLE PAVING OVER EXISTING CONCRETE SURFACE

If your paving is likely to be subjected to heavy traffic, wear and tear, or erosion due to garden sprinkling or rain runoff, you will achieve greater stability by setting the pebbles in mortar over a concrete slab. Mix your mortar with 1 part cement, 2 parts sand, and enough water to give you a mix that doesn't run but spreads easily. Spread a ½-inch layer of the mix over one section of the concrete at a time, placing or sprinkling the pebbles into the area. The pebbles must be wet to give a good bind. When the pebbles have been in place 2 to 3 hours, tamp dry sawdust over the area. After an hour or two, brush off the sawdust with a broom.

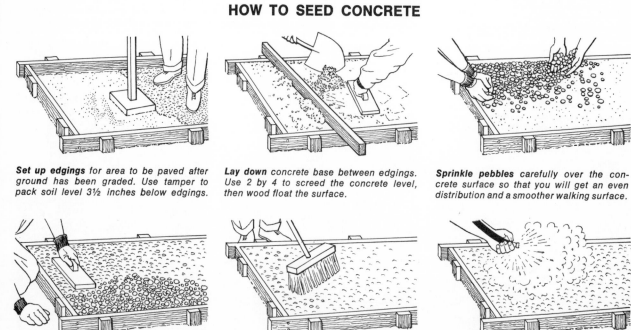

HOW TO SEED CONCRETE

Set up edgings *for area to be paved after ground has been graded. Use tamper to pack soil level 3½ inches below edgings.*

Lay down *concrete base between edgings. Use 2 by 4 to screed the concrete level, then wood float the surface.*

Sprinkle pebbles *carefully over the concrete surface so that you will get an even distribution and a smoother walking surface.*

Press pebbles *into the concrete using a wood float so that the concrete comes to the surface. Let mixture set up a few hours.*

Use brush *to remove loose mortar while concrete is still crumbly. Brush carefully so that pebbles won't completely dislodge.*

Alternate *brushing and washing (use nozzle with fine spray) until the seeded pebbles have been exposed to the desired depth.*

Asphalt paving

Asphalt has long been accepted as a paving for driveways, paths, and service areas, but it also is being used more and more for patio and terrace surfacing because of its low cost. Some homeowners use it in combination with other materials such as brick or concrete.

Because of its flexibility, a 1-inch asphalt pavement will remain intact under light loads in places where concrete would have to be 2 or 3 inches thick simply to hold together.

TWO KINDS OF ASPHALT

The most durable of the two asphalt mixtures is called asphalt concrete. This material is formed by coating heated and dried crushed rock with a hot asphalt cement. The homeowner who attempts to put down this type of asphalt himself usually is not too successful because of the lack of equipment to transport the heated mix. Paving contractors have special equipment for compacting the rock fill and spraying on the hot-mix. They can give you a smooth, level surface that is difficult for the amateur to achieve with limited equipment and lack of know-how.

The other type of asphalt is called cold-mix. It is made by combining graded aggregates with liquid asphalt that has a volatile solvent. When the mixture has been put down as paving, the solvent evaporates, leaving the asphalt cement to hold the aggregates together. For small areas like a path or an extension of a driveway to the house, cold-mix is well worth an attempt by the handyman, and it is useful for patching. But for larger areas, such as a patio, terrace, or large service yard, he

would probably find it difficult to use without a gasoline-driven tamper or a small power roller.

ASPHALT NEEDS A FIRM BASE

Highway engineers know that a pavement is no better than the base on which it is laid. The principle applies in home paving as well. If your ground is sandy or rocky, you may be favored with a good natural base. But if the soil is soft, shows cracks when dry, or is of clay or adobe, put down a base of sand before you pave. A sand base insulates the paving from moisture and mud, which might otherwise work up from below and make the paving unstable.

EDGINGS ARE NECESSARY

Whether you use a hot asphalt or a cold asphalt mix, edgings are required to keep the asphalt from crumbling at the edges. If you decide to have a contractor install a hot mix, you can save on this expense by preparing the ground and installing the edgings yourself. Lumber for the edgings can be as light as finished 1 by 2-inch stock.

ASPHALT CAN BE PAINTED

Asphalt paving may be attractively colored with plastic paints specially manufactured for the purpose. The colors are soft in tone and range from light tan to dark green. Check with your local paint dealer for specific instruction on application.

HOW TO MAKE AN ASPHALT PATH

Spread sand over tamped earth between edgings of 1 by 4's until you have a smooth base about 2 inches deep.

Dump mix from sacks into mounds that are about an inch above the tops of the forms. Space mounds about a foot apart.

Carefully rake asphalt over sand until it is about 2 inches thick at the edges with a crown up to 3 inches at the center.

Brush roller with water so asphalt will not stick to it; roll several times until asphalt is flush with forms at edges.

Sprinkle sand or white gravel over rolled surface to soften dark appearance of asphalt; use crushed brick for color.

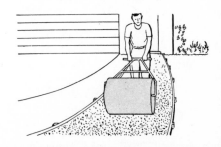

Final rolling insures that gravel or sand is firmly embedded in asphalt. The surface can be walked on right away.

Thirteen choices of garden steps

In constructing steps from house to garden or terrace to terrace, one of the first considerations is the tread and riser relationship. There is a preferred relationship for every situation. If steps are built for a leisurely approach, for example, you'll use one combination; if steps lead to a service area, you'll use a different one. If you want steps that are ideally suited for children, you will cut down on the height of the risers. See the sketch below for the seven best riser and tread combinations.

Below and on the next page are some basic examples of how you can build a garden stairway. None requires perfect finish detail, as plants and foliage will soften the rough edges. There is also no width requirement, but you should figure 4 feet as the minimum for a one-person stairway, 5 feet for a two-person stairway. In many of the examples shown here you can build the risers first, use soil or gravel for temporary treads, and add permanent treads later.

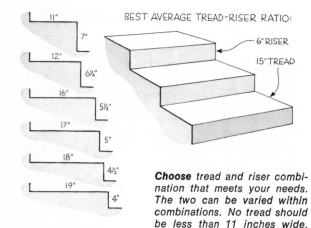

BEST AVERAGE TREAD-RISER RATIO:

Choose tread and riser combination that meets your needs. The two can be varied within combinations. No tread should be less than 11 inches wide.

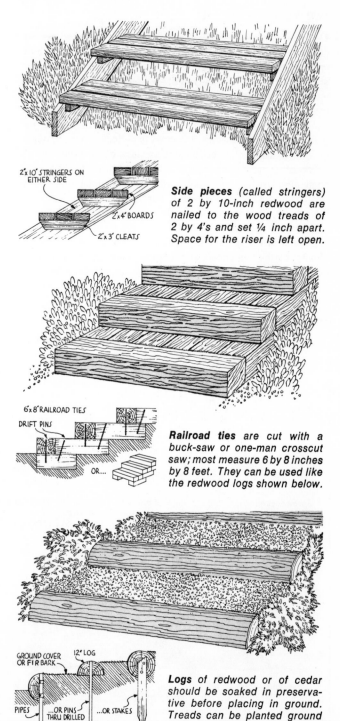

Side pieces (called stringers) of 2 by 10-inch redwood are nailed to the wood treads of 2 by 4's and set ¼ inch apart. Space for the riser is left open.

Treated fir is used for the 2 by 12-inch stringer; cut the stringer to support the 2 by 6-inch risers and treads, each of which are spaced ⅛ to ¼-inch apart.

Railroad ties are cut with a buck-saw or one-man crosscut saw; most measure 6 by 8 inches by 8 feet. They can be used like the redwood logs shown below.

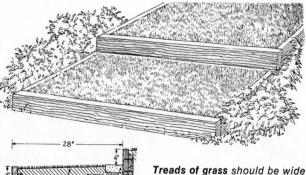

Treads of grass should be wide and broad for ease in cutting. The riser can be made of wood, brick, or of cast concrete; the height of the step is 4 inches.

Logs of redwood or of cedar should be soaked in preservative before placing in ground. Treads can be planted ground cover of dichondra or arenaria.

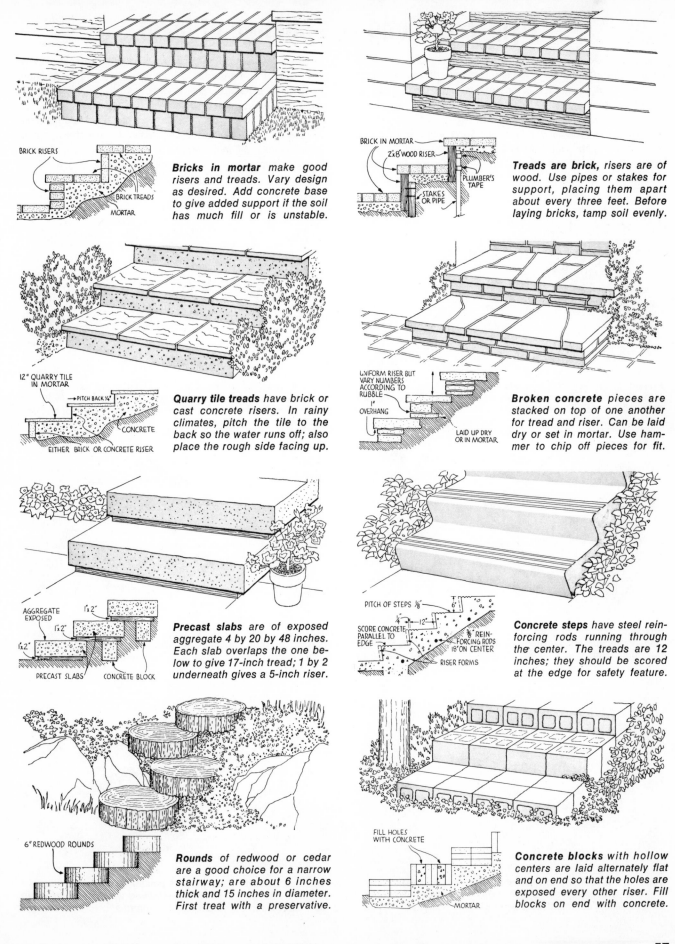

Bricks in mortar make good risers and treads. Vary design as desired. Add concrete base to give added support if the soil has much fill or is unstable.

BRICK RISERS
BRICK TREADS
MORTAR

Treads are brick, risers are of wood. Use pipes or stakes for support, placing them apart about every three feet. Before laying bricks, tamp soil evenly.

BRICK IN MORTAR
2"x8" WOOD RISER
PLUMBER'S TAPE
STAKES OR PIPE

Quarry tile treads have brick or cast concrete risers. In rainy climates, pitch the tile to the back so the water runs off; also place the rough side facing up.

12" QUARRY TILE IN MORTAR
PITCH BACK 1/4"
CONCRETE
EITHER BRICK OR CONCRETE RISER

Broken concrete pieces are stacked on top of one another for tread and riser. Can be laid dry or set in mortar. Use hammer to chip off pieces for fit.

UNIFORM RISER BUT VARY NUMBERS ACCORDING TO RUBBLE
OVERHANG
1"
LAID UP DRY OR IN MORTAR

Precast slabs are of exposed aggregate 4 by 20 by 48 inches. Each slab overlaps the one below to give 17-inch tread; 1 by 2 underneath gives a 5-inch riser.

AGGREGATE EXPOSED
1"x 2"
1"x 2"
1"x 2"
PRECAST SLABS
CONCRETE BLOCK

Concrete steps have steel reinforcing rods running through the center. The treads are 12 inches; they should be scored at the edge for safety feature.

PITCH OF STEPS 1/8"
6"
4"
12"
SCORE CONCRETE PARALLEL TO EDGE
3/8" REINFORCING RODS 18" ON CENTER
RISER FORMS

Rounds of redwood or cedar are a good choice for a narrow stairway; are about 6 inches thick and 15 inches in diameter. First treat with a preservative.

6" REDWOOD ROUNDS

Concrete blocks with hollow centers are laid alternately flat and on end so that the holes are exposed every other riser. Fill blocks on end with concrete.

FILL HOLES WITH CONCRETE
MORTAR

Nine variations in a change of level

The previous two pages discussed various kinds of garden steps that you can build, but did not consider how steps relate to the rest of the garden. Steps are an important part of an entire landscaping plan—frequently they form the focal point about which a garden is planned.

The sketches below show various ways that steps can be used in changing level in a garden. Note that step location and shape are modified in each case to fit different uses for the two

levels. Observe that in each scheme steps are not only an integral part of the garden plan, but have secondary functions as well—to separate areas, to direct foot traffic, to emphasize a key spot in the garden, to hold back soil, to display plantings, to provide extra seating. In each example, the slope has been tailored to fit the stairs and the shape of the stairs has been varied to meet different needs—for fast or leisurely changes in level; for appearance; to make the garden look bigger.

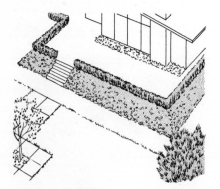

Privacy is gained for the upper terrace through narrow steps and plantings; this helps isolate noise from play area below.

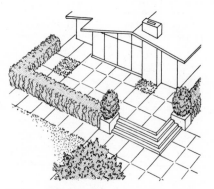

Living center of the garden is reached by the corner steps which invite you to the shade and shelter of the lower level.

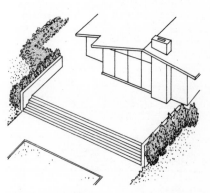

Double duty steps serve as a retaining wall, facilitate the change in level, and give a sense of large-scale dimension.

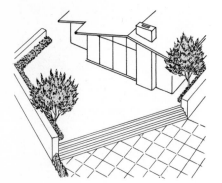

Spacious feeling to entry is achieved with broad, directional steps; also help to direct traffic to the center of garden.

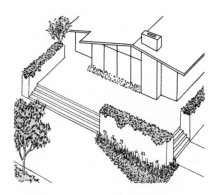

Two sets of steps for different purposes. Broad steps lead from sidewalk to entry, narrow steps provide driveway shortcut.

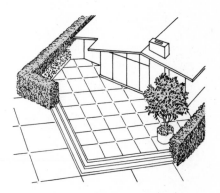

Broad steps project into the lower level; help tie two levels together, especially when activities are spread over both.

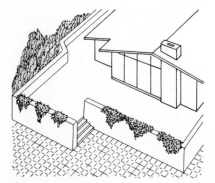

Steps are hidden by low walls to help preserve the privacy of upper terrace; achieve almost complete level separation.

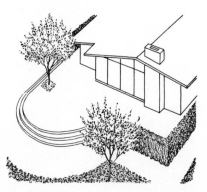

Level below is enhanced by large, curved steps, which offer unlimited routes to the entry, flower bed, driveway, rear garden.

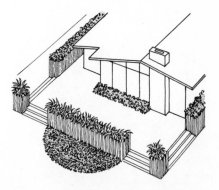

Steps and planter boxes are combined to act as retaining wall for upper level; plantings lend informality to level change.

Garden and patio walls

The purpose and function of a garden or patio wall varies considerably. Some people build a wall for the same reason they build a fence — to provide privacy, to screen off an undesirable view, to act as a boundary line, or to simply define areas within the garden. Others build a wall to delineate a planted area or to hold back a piece of sloping ground.

Whatever the purpose of a wall, certain forms and materials serve certain functions better than others. The following pages give some ideas, some suggestions, and some hints to help you decide which wall may be best for you. A simple low wall can easily be handled by the amateur; high walls (more than 3 feet), however, are best entrusted to a contractor.

Large bricks *create solid wall that blocks street noises. The tree branch comes through the space left open in the bricks.*

Staggered bricks *create a baffle to give privacy to a window close to the entry walk. Design: Baldwin, Eriksson & Peters.*

Concrete blocks *screen carport from the patio. Perforated, solid blocks alternate. Design: Ralph Wyatt, Frank E. Martin.*

Shadow block wall *affords privacy for sunbathers on patio. Ridges on blocks create an interesting pattern of shadows.*

Fitted stones *are laid in mortar to add extra strength to this retaining wall for upper terrace. Design: Thomas Church.*

Exposed aggregate *finish makes the wall blend well with desert. Top was troweled smooth. Design: Guy S. Greene & Assoc.*

Poured concrete wall *can be shaped to any curve or angle; defines a patio area or a flower bed. Design: Thomas Church.*

Adobe blocks *have a natural texture and color that make them blend handsomely with almost any type of garden setting.*

Clay tiles *are set on a base of concrete blocks, separate parking area from patio. Design: Guy S. Greene & Associates.*

Poured concrete walls

An advantage to using poured concrete for a garden wall is that you can have almost any shape that you can build a form for. Also, you can have virtually any surface texture from very smooth to rough or embossed.

BUILDING THE FORMS

Building and aligning the forms for a concrete wall takes more time than the actual pouring. Quite possibly, it may take you as many as three or four weekends to construct the form for a special design. Here are some important points to remember:

1. A wall foundation should be twice the wall width to serve as a footing. It should be laid on firm, hard ground or below frost level in winter climates.

2. Forms should be built with lumber that is free of knotholes and straight. Plywood gives a smooth finish and has good strength. The forms should be braced (see drawing below).

3. Curved forms are usually made of thin plywood or 1-inch lumber that is saw-kerfed on the inward side that is to be curved.

4. The inside of the forms should be brushed with an inexpensive oil so that the concrete will not stick to the walls.

5. Opposite posts should be joined with wire ties to help the form resist the pressure of the concrete. (When the forms are removed, the wire is cut off close to the wall.) Wood spreaders are placed inside the form to hold the sides apart and against the posts, fastening a wire to each spreader so that it can be pulled out as the concrete is being poured.

MIXING AND POURING THE CONCRETE

The recommended formula for mixing concrete for a poured wall is the same as that given for concrete paving (see page 52). Once the concrete is mixed for a wall, it must be poured in continuous layers 6 to 8 inches deep; each layer must be tamped in place with a 2 by 4 or narrow shovel.

Try to complete the entire pouring in one day. Otherwise, you may have a crack or line where the next day's pour joins.

CAPPING THE SURFACE

It's best to cap the top of a concrete wall to prevent rain water from seeping down into it. This is particularly important in areas where winters are severe and where seepage might freeze and crack the concrete. There are three ways to cap a wall: (1) Trowel a fairly stiff mortar (ratio of 1 to 3) on top of the concrete while it is damp and shape it with a curved template. (2) If the wall is to be used as a bench, fasten a redwood plank to the top with 3-inch bolts (see drawing below). The bolts must be set in the concrete while it is still in a plastic state. (3) Apply a masonry sealer after the surface has completely set up.

FORMS ARE LEFT IN PLACE FOR CURING

Once concrete has been poured, it must be kept moist in order for it to set up properly. Use a fine spray over the forms and exposed surface at least twice a day for about a week to 10 days.

HOW TO POUR A CONCRETE WALL

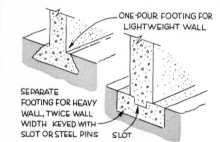

Pour foundation at same time you pour wall if structure is lightweight. Heavier wall usually requires previously poured footing.

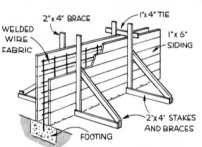

Construct form of wood that is smooth, knot free. Brace with 2 by 4's; place welded wire rods in center to reinforce concrete.

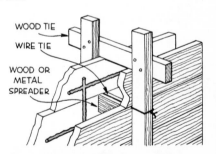

Place spreaders between sides of form to hold them apart. Use wire to join opposite posts, brace against concrete pressure.

Pour concrete using 2 by 4 to tamp in place. Work concrete next to form to force large aggregates away from the surface.

Use wood float to give rough finish to concrete; let water sheen disappear; then use steel trowel to produce smooth finish.

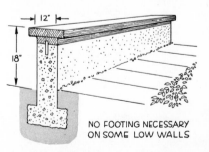

Attach bench seat by using 2 by 6 bolted three inches deep in the concrete. Nail rough or finished 2 by 10 board on top.

Natural-stone walls

Perhaps the most challenging part of building a stone wall is fitting irregular shapes and sizes into a pleasing and effective pattern. A carefully fitted stone wall has a natural sculptured beauty that few other materials can match. Almost any type of stone that is available in quantity can be used. The easiest stones to trim and face are stratified rocks, such as sandstone, limestone, and shale. However, they are not recommended for use in winter climates, where the combination of excess moisture and low temperatures tend to crumble the layered composition of such rocks. The most durable rocks are composed of granite and basalt. Their very toughness, however, makes them harder to break and chip for fitting purposes.

Stone walls can be built with or without mortar. Naturally, the use of mortar will produce a more durable structure, but if stones are properly fitted together, their weight and balance alone are enough to hold them together.

TWO TYPES OF STONEWORK

There are two broad classes of stonework — rubble and ashlar. Rubble masonry is composed of uncut stones, fitted together in their natural state. Ashlar masonry is built with cut stones, laid in fairly regular courses. An amateur may find the ashlar stone

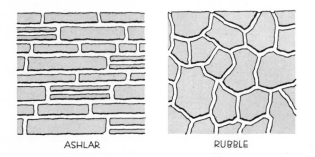

ASHLAR   RUBBLE

easier to use because the regularly shaped stones can be laid in place with less juggling than is required for irregularly shaped rubble stones.

THE QUANTITY AND SIZE OF STONE REQUIRED

The amount of stone required for building a wall is normally figured in tons; the area that a ton will cover will depend on the type of stone used. Your dealer will quickly figure the needed quantity if you provide him with the total cubic wall area.

Be sure to choose a variety of sizes in the type of stone you select; usually the face area of the larger stones should not be more than 5 or 6 times the face area of the smallest stones. The larger stones should be laid in the lower levels, the smaller stones in the upper. Large stones can sometimes be broken to size while you are working.

TOOLS AND EQUIPMENT YOU WILL NEED

The most important tools and equipment you will need are a hammer for chipping stones, a sledge hammer for breaking stones, a container for holding mortar, a spade or shovel for digging the foundation trench, a wheelbarrow for carrying materials, and a trowel for spreading mortar.

In order to keep your work aligned, use a mason's twine or string to mark the boundaries. Also use a level for checking alignment as the work progresses.

AMOUNT OF MORTAR REQUIRED

Because of the numerous and irregular size of joints to be filled, stonework requires a relatively large quantity of mortar. There is no sure way of estimating the amount needed to build a complete wall; however, one solution is to lay up a small section, figure the amount of mortar you used, and then compute the quantity needed for the rest of the wall.

The recommended formula for mortar is 1 part cement and 3 parts clean sand. (For detailed instructions on the actual mixing process for mortar, see the discussion on mixing mortar for brick walls on page 62.)

USE A FOUNDATION FOR ADDED STRENGTH

Any masonry structure should have a foundation of stone or concrete set well below the surface of the ground. Where the climate is mild, a foundation of 10-12 inches depth is usually sufficient for a 3-foot wall. Make sure the ground under the foundation is firm and compact.

A dry wall — one that is assembled without mortar — does not require a deep foundation, even in regions of severe climate. The wall may topple or list a bit, but is easily repaired when good weather comes along.

Concrete foundations are easy to pour (see drawings on the opposite page) and are relatively inexpensive. If a stone foundation is used, it should be laid with mortar, and have time to dry completely before the actual wall construction is started.

PROCEDURE FOR SETTING THE STONES

Before you begin construction of the wall, make sure that you have enough rocks on hand and placed where you can easily reach them as you work. If you have a choice of sizes and shapes, you will be able to keep your pattern interesting. Try placing several stones in a small section before mortaring to see if the pattern is the one you desire. Then begin the construction. Here are some helpful hints to guide you:

1. Remove all dirt and lichen or algae from the stones with water and a stiff brush. (Do not use a steel brush as it may produce rust stains.) Let rocks dry before mortaring.

2. String a guide line to keep the face of the wall flush. Place the first row of stones so they do not jut beyond this line.

3. To give the wall the proper slope inward, nail two boards together at the angle desired, for checking as work progresses. Your wall should slope 1 inch in every 24 inches of height.

4. Offset vertical joints at every course to assure a proper bond. Also set some stones with their long dimensions at right angles to the face of the wall to add strength.

5. Make sure that all joints are completely filled with mortar. Make the joints as thin as possible by filling empty spaces with small chips of stone while filling with mortar.

6. After laying one section, use a stick to rake out the joints on the facing before the mortar sets. The deeper the rake, the better the shadow effect. Brush off excess mortar with an old broom before it completely sets up.

Brick walls

Building a brick wall is involved enough that you will benefit by having had some experience handling the material beforehand, even if you have done no more than lay bricks in sand. Still, there is no substitute for working with mortar and brick. No matter how much you read about handling a trowel you will never quite appreciate the degree of skill involved until you try it yourself. Therefore, it is wise to restrict your first efforts to the building of a low wall (no more than 3 feet high).

WALL THICKNESS A CONSIDERATION

You can build a wall that is 4 inches thick (the width of one brick), providing it is no higher than 2 feet — a higher wall must be wider to withstand lateral pressures. One exception is a curved wall, which forms its own support. (Since each curve is an arc of a circle, in laying out such a wall you merely set up a stake or pole to serve as a center point for a string to form whatever diameter you wish.)

The width of a brick wall higher than 2 feet, or of a high retaining wall, should be 8 inches, and steel reinforcing rods should be used at frequent intervals. If a wall is also of considerable length, it should be reinforced about every 12 feet with a pilaster or brick pier.

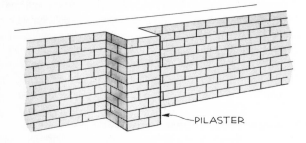
PILASTER

FOUNDATION REQUIREMENTS

The size and type of foundation needed for a brick wall varies with the underlying soil structure, the weight of the wall, and (if a retaining wall) the ground water pressure behind it. If there is any question in your mind about the stability of the wall you plan, it is best to get professional advice before you begin.

For walls up to 2 feet in height the first course of bricks can act as a foundation. Simply dig down to solid ground and set the first course on a bed of mortar. Make this first course twice the width of the wall. Walls that are higher than 2 feet should be set on a concrete foundation.

MIXING THE MORTAR

Everyone has his own favorite mortar mix for brick work. Opinion varies about the proper proportions of cement, lime, and sand, but the following considerations seem to be universally recognized. The more lime in the mix, the easier it is to work; it is more plastic, holds water better, sticks to the trowel better, but has less strength. The more cement in the mix, the harder it is to work; it may be granular and lumpy, and won't stick to the trowel, but it's stronger.

A good all-around mortar mix is 1 part cement, 1 to 1¼ parts

hydrated lime or lime putty (lime in a plastic state), and 5 or 6 parts loose, damp sand.

For very small jobs, you can buy ready-to-mix mortar to which you just add water, or sand and water.

For the actual mixing, you will need a flat surface such as a square of plywood, a wooden box, or an old wheelbarrow. Mix all the dry ingredients thoroughly with a short-handled, square-edged shovel or a garden hoe. Then add water slowly. The mortar should be just wet enough to slide cleanly off the mixing tool or a trowel but it should not be runny. Mix mortar in small batches so it won't dry out.

TOOLS AND EQUIPMENT

The most important tools for brick laying are the pointed trowel with a 10-inch blade, for spreading the mortar, and a broad-bladed cold chisel called a "brick set," for cutting bricks. Other

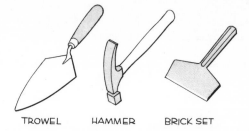
TROWEL   HAMMER   BRICK SET

tools that you are likely to need are a hammer, a carpenter's square, a length of fishing line, a piece of straight wood about 5 feet long and a level.

SETTING THE BRICKS IN MORTAR

Before applying any mortar to the bricks, lay an unmortared test row on the foundation to check the fit, leaving a ½ inch opening between each brick for the mortar joint. Space the openings until the bricks fill the guide lines properly, then you can set them in place with mortar.

Pick up some mortar on the trowel and spread it on the base about ½ inch thick, working from left to right. Turn the trowel over and use a zigzag motion (called furrowing) to work the

mortar out to the edge. Pick up a brick in your free hand, "butter" one end with mortar, and set it in place. Push it down into the mortar bed until the mortar squeezes out the sides. Scrape off this excess mortar and use it to butter the next brick.

When the first course of bricks is in place, build up the ends or corners of the wall (see sketch on the opposite page). Attach a guide line to these corners (such as a good quality fishing line), using nails in the mortar joints. Use a length of straight

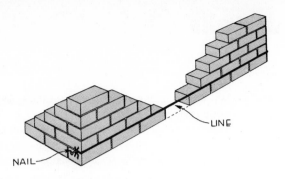

LINE

NAIL

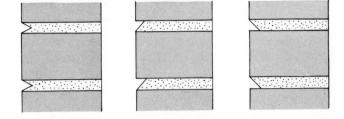

professional striking tool. The joint made with the trowel handle held down is preferred by many because of its water-shedding ability and because each course of bricks will throw a pleasing shadow effect that runs horizontally along the wall.

wood to check that the end bricks are plumb. Then complete laying each course moving the guide line up as you work.

STRIKING THE MORTAR JOINTS

For a professional-looking finish, trim off any loose mortar and smooth off the joints before the mortar completely sets up. Smooth the vertical joints first, then the horizontal. The most popular method is to use a short piece of steel pipe with a diameter slightly larger than the joint. By drawing the pipe along the mortar joint, you produce a smooth, concave surface. Some other methods for striking mortar joints are with the edge of a board; with the handle of the trowel held down; with the handle of the trowel held up; with the tip of the trowel; with a

CLEAN WITH MURIATIC ACID

For the first two or three days after completing your brick wall, it is a good idea to keep it wet with an occasional fine spray from a hose. This helps speed the setting-up action. Wait a period of two to three weeks to see if any white efflorescence (excess water rising to the surface of the brick) appears over the brickwork. Efflorescence and any smears of mortar can be removed with a mild solution of muriatic acid. This chemical is extremely potent and should be handled with care. For detailed instructions on the application of this solution, see the discussion on paving with bricks on page 48.

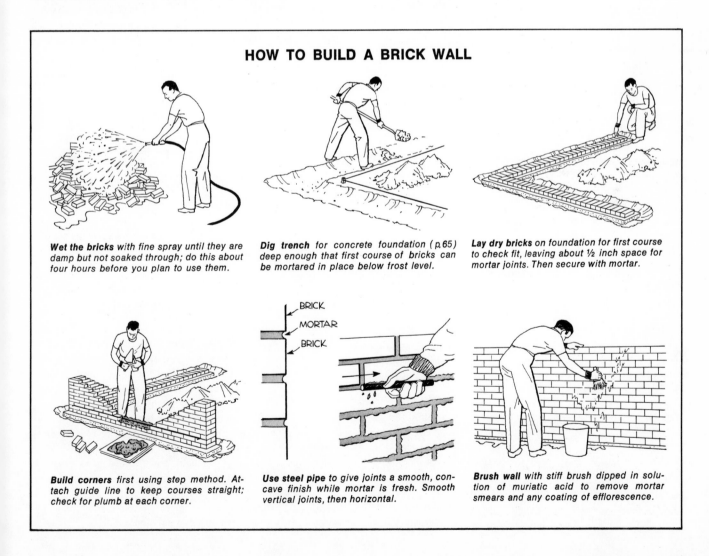

HOW TO BUILD A BRICK WALL

Wet the bricks with fine spray until they are damp but not soaked through; do this about four hours before you plan to use them.

Dig trench for concrete foundation (p.65) deep enough that first course of bricks can be mortared in place below frost level.

Lay dry bricks on foundation for first course to check fit, leaving about ½ inch space for mortar joints. Then secure with mortar.

Build corners first using step method. Attach guide line to keep courses straight; check for plumb at each corner.

BRICK
MORTAR
BRICK

Use steel pipe to give joints a smooth, concave finish while mortar is fresh. Smooth vertical joints, then horizontal.

Brush wall with stiff brush dipped in solution of muriatic acid to remove mortar smears and any coating of efflorescence.

Concrete block walls

Building a garden or patio wall with concrete blocks is perhaps the easiest approach for the beginner — it also is fast. The size of the blocks alone (8 by 8 by 16) makes a wall go together much more quickly and smoothly than with bricks.

There are two basic types of concrete blocks used for building walls: heavyweight and lightweight. A heavyweight block is made with the same ingredients as used in ordinary concrete; a lightweight block is composed of such aggregates as volcanic lava, clay or shale, cinders, and often pumice. The latter has a more porous texture than the "true concrete" block, but offers better insulation.

Most concrete blocks come in two sizes: 8 by 8 by 16, or 4 by 8 by 16. They also come with three or two core holes.

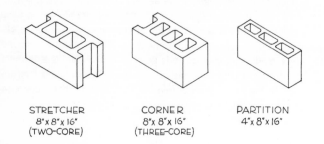

STRETCHER
8"x 8"x 16"
(TWO-CORE)

CORNER
8"x 8"x 16"
(THREE-CORE)

PARTITION
4"x 8"x 16"

THE USE OF DECORATIVE BLOCKS

In recent years a wide selection of decorative shapes and textures for concrete blocks has become available. You can select blocks that look like rough-cut stones or flagstone slabs. You can buy a variety called slumped block or Slumpstone; the face of each block has individual contours. A wall built of slumped rock gives the appearance of being made of weathered stone or adobe.

One of the most striking of the decorative blocks is screen block, each of which is an individual grillework. Using various combinations, you can build a highly stylized wall.

CHOICE OF FOUNDATIONS

A concrete block wall may be laid on a dry concrete foundation or a wet concrete foundation. A dry foundation is one that has been allowed to set up; a wet foundation is still in a plastic state. The latter produces a sturdier wall but is harder to work with as you must pour the footing and start laying blocks all in one working session. For the week-end handyman, it is better to rely on transit mix for the footing, then proceed to set the blocks on the base as soon as it is firm. Following are some helpful hints for both types of foundations.

Dry foundation. After the poured foundation has set up (2 to 3 days), check on the positioning of the blocks by fitting a dry first course on the foundation. Keep a space between the blocks of about ½ inch. Mark the position of each block and lay it aside.

Mix mortar following the directions given on page 62. Wet the foundation. Use a trowel to spread 2 inches of mortar over the foundation, place a damp block on the mixture, and tap it

firmly with the trowel handle until it is securely embedded in mortar.

Wet foundation. Before pouring the footing, check the positioning of the blocks by laying out a test row alongside the foundation trench. Then pour the concrete footing and let it set up until it is the consistency of mortar. Set the blocks in place, pressing them into the mix until they are embedded about 2 inches deep.

Set succeeding courses by troweling mortar along the edges of the first course. Put blocks in place, tapping each with the trowel handle to give it a firm bedding.

No matter what type of foundation you use, the top course of the wall must be sealed against water penetration by filling in the hollow cores with a mixture of grout — 1 part cement and 5 parts sand. (You can add coarse gravel to extend this mixture.) After the holes have been filled, cap the surface with a coping of wood, brick, or concrete block veneer attached with a smooth layer of sand-and-cement grout.

REINFORCING RODS NEEDED FOR HIGHER WALLS

For a wall greater than 4 feet high, set vertical reinforcing rods solidly in the concrete foundation while it is still plastic, spacing them so they will fit through the holes of the blocks in each course. If you use a wet foundation, simply drive the rods through the block holes after laying the first course. The holes surrounding the rods in each course must be filled with a mixture of grout and gravel.

USE EPOXY MORTAR TO SET SCREEN BLOCK

Because of their make-up and design, screen blocks lack the solidity of ordinary concrete blocks and therefore require a stronger type mortar than is normally used in construction. Epoxy mortar gives an incredibly hard joint, so hard, in fact, that it is much easier to break the block than the joint. Once the wall is completed, the joint is almost invisible.

Epoxy costs about twice as much as ordinary mortars. It consists of two components (available from brick or block manufacturers) which you mix together just before using it.

With epoxy mortar, you usually do not have to reinforce a wall unless it exceeds 8 feet in height. If you need to reinforce, steel rods cannot be used because they will show with most screen block designs. Instead give horizontal reinforcing by using strips of wire mesh between each course.

HOW TO BUILD A CONCRETE BLOCK WALL

This step-by-step procedure for building a concrete block wall is designed to guide the amateur wall builder who is attempting the task all alone. Followed carefully, it will help you to build a wall that has all the earmarks of being put together by a professional. Once the preliminary work of digging the foundation trench, building the form, and pouring the foundation is out of the way, you can concentrate on laying the blocks in place. At first you may find this awkward going, but by the time you are ready for the third or fourth course, the work should progress smoothly.

Be sure to mix only enough mortar that can be used before it starts to set up. Otherwise, you will spend much unnecessary time adding water and re-mixing. Also be sure to check that each block is completely level and that it is lined up and plumb with blocks in the course below.

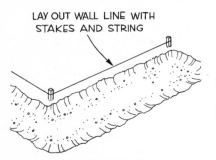

LAY OUT WALL LINE WITH STAKES AND STRING

Foundation trench should be twice as wide as wall width and deep enough that concrete footing rests on solid ground.

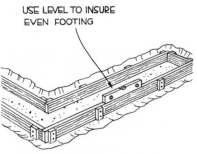

USE LEVEL TO INSURE EVEN FOOTING

Build form for footing at least 6 inches deep and 2 inches below level of the ground. Width should be 4 inches greater than wall.

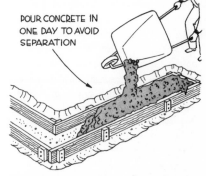

POUR CONCRETE IN ONE DAY TO AVOID SEPARATION

Pour concrete into form using a shovel to spread it into empty spaces and corners. Screed it level with form tops using 2 by 4.

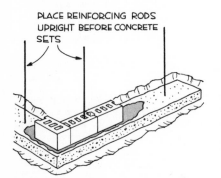

PLACE REINFORCING RODS UPRIGHT BEFORE CONCRETE SETS

Spread mortar over footing 2 inches deep. Place row of blocks so that they are evenly spaced and are level and straight.

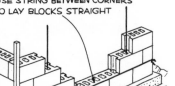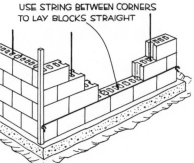

USE STRING BETWEEN CORNERS TO LAY BLOCKS STRAIGHT

Use end blocks to build up corners first. Check for plumb with length of board marked at block height.

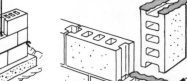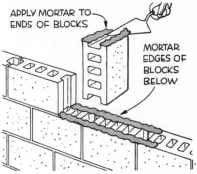

APPLY MORTAR TO ENDS OF BLOCKS

MORTAR EDGES OF BLOCKS BELOW

Butter one end of block to be set in place. Apply ribbons of mortar on the edges of the blocks in the course below.

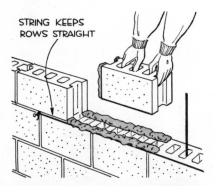

STRING KEEPS ROWS STRAIGHT

Pick up block and firmly place the buttered end against the last block placed in line. String keeps the courses straight.

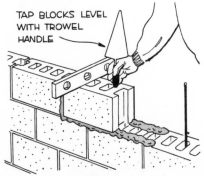

TAP BLOCKS LEVEL WITH TROWEL HANDLE

Use trowel handle to tap blocks level. Check to see that edge of block is in line with string. Scrape off excess mortar.

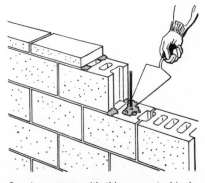

Cap top course with thin concrete blocks after filling each hole with a strong mixture of grout. Tool joints for neat finish.

Courtesy of Permanente Cement Company

Retaining walls

If you live on a hillside lot or have specific areas with a considerable slope to them, retaining walls and earth cutting and filling may be necessary in your landscaping and building plans. One of the most important considerations is drainage. During a rainy season, sloping soil absorbs a large quantity of water, which flows downhill below the surface. When the water reaches a barrier, such as a retaining wall or foundation, it builds up a great amount of pressure that may eventually weaken or break the structure. Ditches, gutters, drain tile, and proper planting can be combined to divert both surface and subsurface water. Weep holes and backfill also help.

You not only must have a building permit, but would be well advised to seek professional help from your local building department before making any attempt at building a retaining wall. If the wall is to be more than four feet high, or if extensive fill is needed, the department may ask for soil tests and a licensed engineer's calculations before it will issue a permit. If you are building a wall no more than four feet high, a masonry wall such as the one shown in the sketch at right should be sufficient to pass inspection and provide the required safety. Other materials you might use for a low retaining wall include pre-cast concrete, cribbing, railroad ties, or poured concrete. Field stone laid in mortar, broken concrete, or rubble walls are not recommended except for low walls not subjected to excessive water pressure. If you do want a stone or rubble wall, it is sometimes best to build an 8-inch-thick, reinforced masonry wall, then add stone facing. The sketches below show various construction methods for building a retaining wall using different materials.

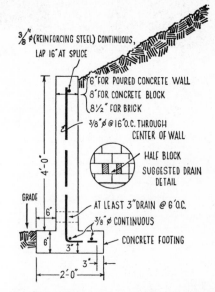

Detail drawing can be used for masonry, brick, or concrete block wall. Drain pipes embedded in masonry or brick openings.

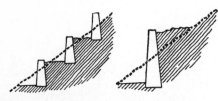

Stepped concrete forms a series of low terraces; these are less likely to lean or to topple down-hill than is one high wall.

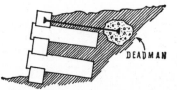

Cast concrete posts can be anchored with keyed posts run back into bank or with rods embedded in mass of concrete.

Poured concrete walls should have extending foot on the downhill side, with reinforcement rods curved into the foot.

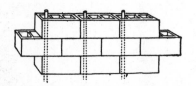

Concrete blocks are offset and reinforced with vertical steel rods. Use grout to fill in the holes surrounding the rods.

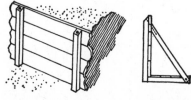

Redwood or cedar is naturally resistant to rot, insect attacks. Wall of 4 by 4's and planks should have each post braced.

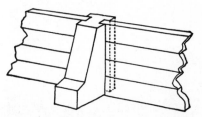

Planks and concrete posts make a strong wall. Post grooves hold ends of treated redwood planks which are slid into place.

Mortared bricks are set on solid footing, and staggered gradually inward with each course. Leave weep holes every 5 feet.

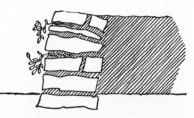

Dry wall of stone holds low banks successfully; can be laid with earth pockets in between. Pitch wall in toward the bank.

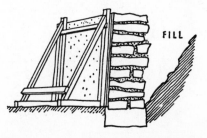

Cut stones are laid in mortar to provide added strength. Use an angle jig of boards to batter the face of the wall.

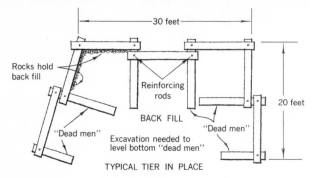

Railroad ties *are set back slightly in a stair-step fashion for greater strength. At the ends the ties are pinned together with reinforcing rods. Space between the ties is blocked with rocks.*

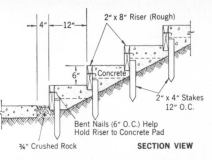

Entire slope *of steep garden is terraced with 2 by 8's, serving both as step risers and as low retaining walls. Stakes supporting risers are spaced every 12 inches; concrete used for treads.*

Cedar strips *covering concrete wall are nailed to the furring strips which have been fastened to the wall with concrete nails; the strips can be stained or left to weather naturally.*

Redwood planks *and posts form a retaining wall four feet high. 2 by 12's are used for capping and to form edging below for herb garden. Gravel, drain tile are placed at wall base behind.*

Basic supporting elements for a deck

Plans for deck construction are usually based on two main themes: a great number of support posts capped with a simple horizontal structure, or a fewer number of posts supporting a sturdier horizontal platform. For example, a ground-hugging deck may have a random number of footings and not be unsightly, whereas a hillside deck requires a few well-placed supports that are solidly anchored but that do not detract from a pleasing visual design. The discussion below is confined to locating and building of footings, use of post connectors, and types and sizes of support posts. (See next two pages for a discussion on support beams, joists, ledger, and deck patterns.)

CONCRETE FOOTING REQUIRED FOR MOST DECKS

A footing made of solid concrete is required by most building codes to anchor a deck securely to its site. For a ground-hugging deck, you can use simple concrete blocks put down on tamped earth, or set on a concrete pad. Pre-cast concrete piers are also available. These piers are usually 12 inches square at the base, 6 inches square at the top, and 12 inches deep. They should be seated on compact soil or a concrete pad.

For hillside decks, the concrete footing should be a foot or more across and extend 18 to 30 inches below grade. You can cast such footings using forms made of wood, metal, or even

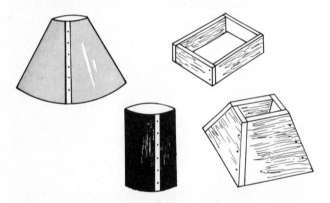

tarpaper. The recommended formula for mixing a concrete footing is 1 part cement, 2 parts clean sand, and 3 parts gravel. An easier method of casting your own footings is to use transit mix. Almost as easy but more expensive is dry mix to which you just add water.

THE PLACEMENT OF FOOTINGS

Close accuracy and placement of footings is an essential part of deck building. The weight of the deck must be evenly distributed over the support posts and the ground. By using the 3-4-5 rule, any difficulty or errors in the "squaring off" is automatically avoided: First, establish a base point (if the deck is to be attached to a house wall, use the wall as the base point). Measure along the wall a distance of three feet and mark a second point (B). Then tie a string to the base point (A) and run it out to reach the outside edge of the deck. At a distance of 4 feet out along this line, mark a third point (C). Then measure between the points B and C and if the distance is exactly 5 feet, the line is at a perfect right angle to the wall. Measure in the same way for each critical footing.

To use the 3-4-5 rule for a detached deck, drive stakes in a straight line to form one edge of the deck and use one of them as your base point.

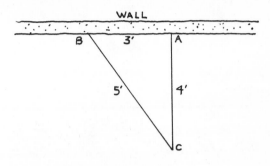

THE USE OF POST CONNECTORS

In order to provide a flat, level surface on which the support posts will rest solidly, one of the three types of post connectors shown below could be used. The simplest and least expensive method is the wood block (B) that is set in the top of the footing while the concrete is still in a plastic state. This method is adequate for short posts, which are then toe-nailed to the block. Another method is to extend a metal pin through the wood block before it is set in the wet concrete (C). After a hole is drilled in the post to accept the pin, toe-nail the post to the wood block. A stronger method of anchoring posts is to use metal fasteners (A). Designed to withstand great stress, they are most commonly used with hillside decks. The long prongs of the metal fasteners are seated in the wet concrete and the top part is bolted to the posts.

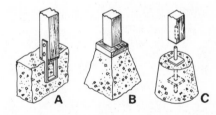

CHOICE OF TYPES AND SIZES FOR SUPPORT POSTS

The most commonly used material for support posts is wood (although concrete and steel can also be used). The 4 by 4 post is adequate for most low decks as it will bear a load of 8,000 pounds up to a height of 8 feet. Larger posts are required for a steep hillside or where the deck is to bear such heavy loads as large groups of people, numerous plant containers and pieces of furniture, or several inches of wet snow. Your local building department will tell you the size required for the type of deck you are building.

Besides the regular sized posts, you can also use a built-up post. These offer a compromise between structural demands and graceful appearance. The sketch on the opposite page illustrates three variations. There is no lack of strength if the separate members are properly joined with heavy nails or screws or bolts.

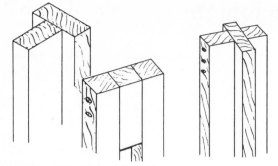

MEASURING FOR POST HEIGHT

Accurate measurement of post heights is an important phase in building a deck. Without it, you cannot build a sub-structure that is stable enough to support a horizontal platform. There are two methods for measuring, each with the same first step as follows: Find and mark a line on the house wall that is even with the top of the deck surface. Measure down the thickness of the decking plus joists to find the top of your ledger. Establish the line, check for level, then snap a chalk line to mark it. Then use either of the following two methods for measuring post height:

Method 1. Set a post in place, check for plumb, and brace it temporarily. Then run a line from the top of the ledger to establish a mark on the post that is even with the top of the ledger. From that mark, subtract the depth of the support beam you will be using and make a new mark. Use a piece of scrap lumber and a carpenter's level to check for line level. Then take down the post and cut off the excess.

Method 2. Rather than setting up the post temporarily, you can measure the length by this mathematical procedure: Establish the ledger line as in method 1, measure down to the ground line of the house to establish a base line. From the base, run a line level out to a footing and measure how far above or below the house line each footing comes. Then take the distance between the base line and the ledger line, subtract the beam thickness, and add or subtract the difference between the footing and the base line. Measure each post in this manner.

CROSS BRACING MAY BE NECESSARY

Some type of cross bracing may be required to prevent vertical movement of the deck. This is particularly true where the deck is built on a steep hillside and the posts are of extra length. The simplest kind of bracing is to use a heavy duty connector between post and beam. Several are described on the following page.

Floor-level deck is supported by concrete blocks. Decking runs at right angle to the house. Design: Armstrong & Sharfman.

Streetside deck rests on posts connected to pre-cast concrete piers. Surface is 2 by 6-inch planks. Design: Elizabeth Dana.

Deck overlooks recreation area below. The deck surface is supported by 4 by 8 posts and beams. Design: Terry and Moore.

Concrete columns support framework of heavy 4 by 10-inch underpinning of the deck. Design: Glen Hunt & Associates.

Deck beams and joists

Most building codes require that a deck be designed to bear 40 pounds of weight per square foot. This figure applies mainly to the beam and joist construction—the size and span of the members and the methods of anchoring in place. The size and weight of the beam required depends entirely on its span and spacing. A good rule in general is that the depth of the beam in inches may be equalled in feet of span (a 6-inch beam can span 6 feet). Joists are normally of 2-inch dimensions and are required to support the deck surface and whatever loads are placed on that surface. The joist span is determined by the joist and beam spacing and the grade of lumber.

METHODS OF SECURING BEAMS

Once the beam is set squarely on top of the post, there are several methods for anchoring it in place (see drawing below). The simplest approach is toe-nailing (A), but is normally used for small, ground-hugging decks. A stronger method is to use strap metal which comes in straight pieces, L shapes, or T shapes (B, C, D).

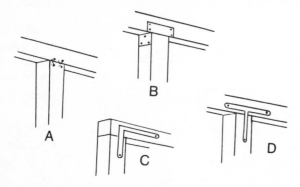

METHODS OF SECURING JOISTS

Since joists individually bear a lesser load than do beams, they can be placed on top of the beams or attached flush with their tops (see drawing below). The stronger method is the first. If the joists are seated on top of the beams, toe-nailing them in place will be adequate (A). If you want the joists to be set flush with the beams, it is best to use an angle iron or joist hanger

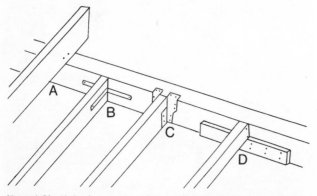

(B and C). If the beams are deeper than the joist, tack a ledger strip of wood to the beam and rest the smaller member on it and toe-nail in place (D).

JOINING BEAM OR JOIST ENDS

If the length of one beam is not enough to span the length or width of the deck, you will be required to join two beams. This joint should be directly over a post. The same is true with joining a joist. Each end of the member should have a resting surface of at least 1 inch on the supporting member. Toe-nail the

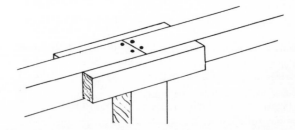

ends together on the top and nail heavy scabs (scrap pieces of lumber) on both sides. The scabs should equal the depth of the member and be at least 2 feet long.

CROSS-BRACING JOISTS

Lateral bracing for joists is usually required if the ratio of the width to the depth is less than 1:2. For example, a 2 by 4 (ratio of 1 to 2) does not need bracing, but a 2 by 6 (ratio of 1 to 3) requires bracing to prevent its twisting or buckling.

There are two easy methods for bracing. The first method uses pieces of 2 by 4 nailed in crosswise fashion (see drawing below) at regular intervals. For an 8-foot span, cross-bracing at either end is sufficient. If the span is at least 15 feet or more, use this bracing method every 2 feet.

The second method is to use spacer blocks between the joists at or near their ends. The spacers should equal the depth of the joists and be toe-nailed in place.

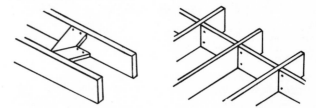

ATTACHING LEDGERS

A ledger is a 2 by 4, 2 by 6, or other plank nailed or bolted to a house wall to support the surface boards of a deck or the deck joists. Ledgers can be attached to the studs of wood walls with either nails or expansion screws. Once you have located the height of the ledger, snap a chalk line to mark it. If the ledger is fairly long, it is a good idea to nail several pieces of scrap lumber on the wall to support the ledger while you are nailing it in place. Start your first nail or screw at the center of the ledger; then tack each end. Check with a level to make sure it hasn't slipped. Use two or more nails or lags at each stud.

If you are attaching the ledger to a masonry wall, use expansion bolts. Make a mark for the bolts about 16 inches apart, and use an electric drill with a masonry bit to drill a hole at least 2 inches into the wall. Insert the expansion shield in the hole and secure the ledger with the bolts, including washers.

Deck patterns

There is a wide range of possible patterns for decking. The two simplest patterns are to lay the decking parallel to a wall, or at right angles to it. These patterns require no modification of beam and joist construction.

DIAGONAL PATTERNS

This pattern of decking may be laid on a diagonal to the joists, at any angle greater than 45°. It is often used to relieve the monotony of the normal square or rectangularly shaped decks, or to give a distinctive shape to the deck. Standard framing is used for this pattern, but it should be noted that the diagonal decking spans are greater and the joists may have to be set closer together than would be necessary with standard pattern decking. It should also be noted that if one side of the deck follows the diagonal, an edging or facing should be attached to the joist ends to help support the decking.

GEOMETRIC SHAPES AND FREE FORMS

These variations of standard or diagonal decking patterns include triangles, hexagons, circles, and curves. Almost any form or shape can be achieved as long as the joists are closely spaced and a braced joist lies near the edge of the deck.

PARQUET AND DIAMOND PATTERN DECKS

These sectional patterns of a deck require a grid pattern of support which is achieved by using block supports between the joists at a distance equal to the joist spacing. If the joists are of 2-inch dimension, the support blocks should also be of 2-inch dimension. The exception to the framing requirements of this pattern is when it is laid directly on concrete or sand. In this instance, a framework of 2 by 4's will be adequate for support and nailing the deck surface in place.

FRAMING AROUND TREES

The planning of either low-level or high-level decks may necessitate provisions for encircling a tree. Both framing and decking must allow ample clearance for trunk growth and for possible swaying in a strong wind.

The various deck patterns shown below are courtesy of the California Redwood Association.

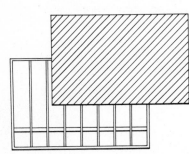
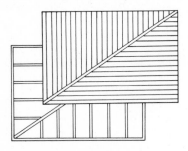
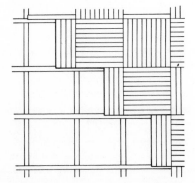
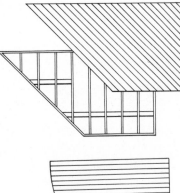
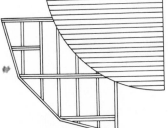
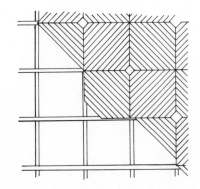
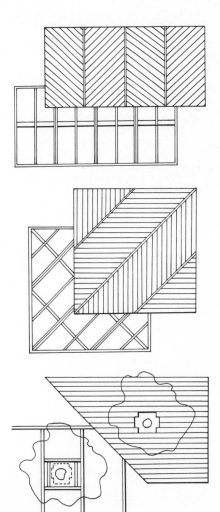

STEP-BY-STEP CONSTRUCTION OF A DECK

After you have decided what type of deck you want and its exact location, be sure to take your building plan to your local building inspector for review. He may have some suggestions for change in design or materials that may not only save some money for you but also time and effort. Then, after receiving a building permit, you can begin to prepare the site for actual construction.

There are three basic steps for preparing a site to receive a deck: soil preparation, grading, and drainage.

Clear the soil of weeds and unnecessary growth. Then cover the area with builder's paper or plastic sheeting held in place with a thin layer of gravel. An alternative method of weed control is to spray the area with a weed killer. You can buy selective weed killers, temporary soil sterilants, and permanent sterilants. An experienced nurseryman or gardener will help you in choosing one for your particular situation.

Normally, it is not necessary to grade a site before building a deck, but when it is the job is usually minor. Some sloping lots may need a few high spots leveled to permit setting a deck at indoor floor level.

Or, a particularly bumpy site may require some smoothing out. Be sure to avoid digging too deep.

Drainage problems are more likely to occur on a flat lot than on a sloping or hillside lot. Often there are spots that are slightly lower than the rest of the ground and that remain too soggy for comfortable use for days after a rain. A dry well at this low point may solve the problem but care must be taken not to disturb the soil around the hole. A safer and easier way is to dig a ditch that slopes away to good drainage. The ditch should be at least a foot deep, and should drop at least 1 inch each 15 feet. Then lay 4-inch sewer tile on its floor with the joints loosely fitted together. Cover the tile with drain rock and on top of it a layer of builder's paper. Then fill the ditch with dirt to grade level.

When all of these three considerations have been taken care of you are ready to begin construction of your deck. While the series of steps below may not match your building plan exactly, it will guide you through the general steps involved in building any deck.

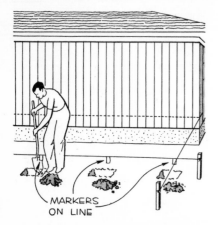

Dig holes for post footings to proper depth following guide lines that have been set so they will not get in the way when you are ready to pour the concrete.

Place pier forms in position over holes. Make sure they are level with each other by checking with a line level or carpenter's level. Then fill the form with concrete.

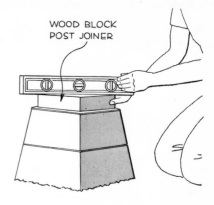

Place post joiner in the wet concrete. Use level to make sure it is horizontally and vertically level. If deck is built on hillside, use metal joiner for added strength.

Use chalk line to establish desired level of the deck. Level the chalk line and snap to mark the position of ledger. Nail the ledger in place starting at center.

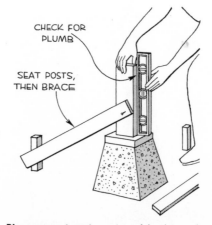

Place support posts on top of footing and wood joiner. Use scrap lumber to brace posts while you check for plumb with carpenter's level on two adjacent sides.

Check level of support beam to make sure all the posts in the row are on an even plane. A short post can be built up with a shingle wedge; a long one needs to be cut.

Check horizontal alignment for ledger and beams by measuring out from ledger; measure at both ends and in the middle. Deck should slope downward for drainage.

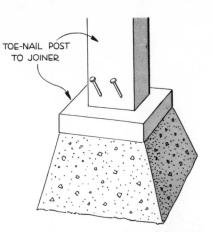

TOE-NAIL POST TO JOINER

Secure post to wood joiner once level is assured in each direction using toe-nailing method. For metal joiner, use special nails included, following directions.

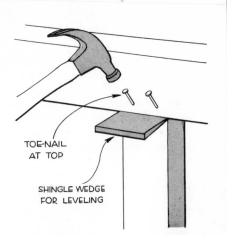

TOE-NAIL AT TOP

SHINGLE WEDGE FOR LEVELING

Place beam on support posts and nail in place using toe-nailing method. To prevent against possible wind lift, use a metal connector or strap metal of any form.

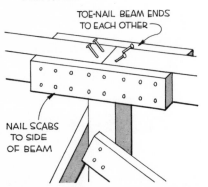

TO FORM END JOINTS OVER A POST:

TOE-NAIL BEAM ENDS TO EACH OTHER

NAIL SCABS TO SIDE OF BEAM

Brace beam joints over a post by toe-nailing the two ends to each other, then nail scabs heavily in place on either side. Scabs should be at least 2 feet long.

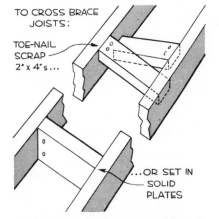

TO CROSS BRACE JOISTS:

TOE-NAIL SCRAP 2" x 4"s...

...OR SET IN SOLID PLATES

Cross brace joists with pieces of 2 by 4's or scrap lumber. They do not need to be nailed as heavy as beam. To prevent buckling, use either method shown above.

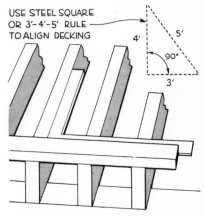

USE STEEL SQUARE OR 3'-4'-5' RULE TO ALIGN DECKING

Use steel square or 3-4-5 rule (see page 68) to assure that decking will be true. Once first board is straight, others can be forced into line in pattern you desire.

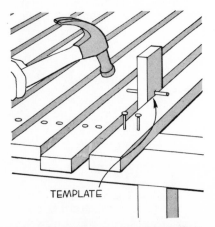

TEMPLATE

Nail boards at each bearing surface. Keep nails in straight lines for neat appearance. Use scrap of wood for template to assure an even spacing between the boards.

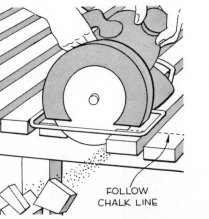

FOLLOW CHALK LINE

Trim edges of boards following chalked line. Apply a coat of sealer to the ends and to any dents from hammering. Paint or stain complete deck surface as desired.

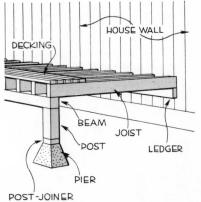

HOUSE WALL

DECKING

BEAM

POST

JOIST

LEDGER

PIER

POST-JOINER

Completed view illustrates the primary components for a low-level or simple hillside deck attached to a house wall. Plan can be adapted to other typical designs.

Barbecues and firepits

Most landscape architects will agree that a barbecue doesn't have to be a garden monument in order to be efficient. Size alone means little. The thing that matters is whether the unit will perform efficiently without straining the owner's pocketbook and without overpowering other features of the garden or patio.

For many people, buying a portable unit is the answer rather than trying to fit one of masonry into the established surroundings. However, you may have only one suitable location and feel that it is practical to build a permanent structure. The five units shown on these two pages are built of masonry. Each one can be used as a barbecue or as a firepit. Type and style varies but techniques for building are the same. If you are unfamiliar with brick masonry, it would be well worth your while to check the sections in this book on brick paving and building brick walls for the basic procedures involved and the type of mortar mix required.

A BARBECUE-FIREPIT COMBINATION

Firepit, brick paving, and garden seat are brought together in one continuous unit. Bricks used in the firepit should be firebrick (hard-burned red brick). Barbecue grill is held rigid at various heights by iron pins (reinforcing rods).

Design: C. Mason Whitny, R. Burton Litton, Jr., Robert J. Tetlow.

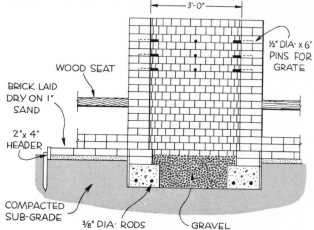

BARBECUE GRILL TURNS ON LONG SCREW

The grill on this barbecue turns on a long screw and can be raised to 12 inches above the brazier. The brazier rests on a masonry base — use any material in harmony with other masonry in your patio. A long workbench vise screw supports the grill.

Design: A. K. Tobin.

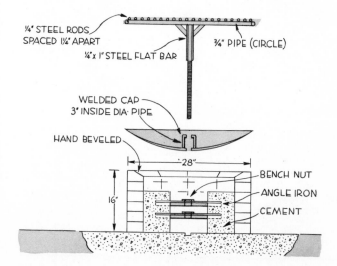

GRILL COVERS FIREPIT WHEN NOT IN USE

When not in use, the opening of this firepit can be covered with a grill for a safety feature. Bricks are laid in mortar containing fireclay to prevent cracking. Base of sand and gravel helps drainage. For small fires, you could use common brick set at grade level for the ring, and firebricks for the pit lining.

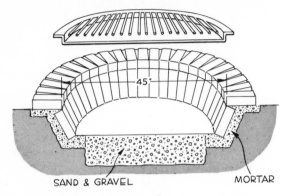

45"

SAND & GRAVEL   MORTAR

FIREPIT IN CONCRETE - PAVED PATIO

Five-foot-wide firepit in concrete-paved patio provides friendly gathering place. Circle contains 39 Roman bricks set in mortar. Two layers of gravel provide for drainage. Guests can barbecue over a bed of coals using long-handled forks or skewers.

Design: Arnold Dutton.

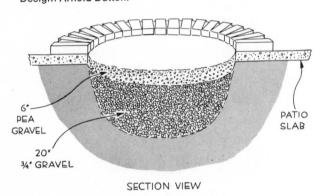

6" PEA GRAVEL

20" ¾" GRAVEL

PATIO SLAB

SECTION VIEW

TABLE-TOP COVERS FIREPIT

The table top that fits inside this firepit is made of five redwood 2 by 6's and two 2 by 8's nailed to a circle of exterior plywood. Metal legs are 16 inches long. The circle of bricks has outside diameter of 38¾ inches. Pit is 18½ inches deep, and is lined with firebrick below patio level.

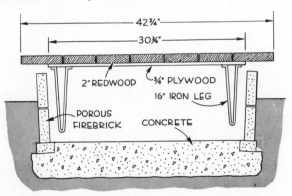

42¾"

30¾"

2" REDWOOD   ¾" PLYWOOD

16" IRON LEG

POROUS FIREBRICK   CONCRETE

Low-voltage garden lighting

Often heralded as a new development is low-voltage (l-v) lighting. It's really not new — for decades it has been used for automobiles — but in a garden it is a relatively new concept and, with today's equipment, it can bring exciting advantages.

One of the most important advantages is safety. If a child removes the bulb from any 12-volt garden light fixture and pokes his fingers inside, he won't receive a dangerous electrical shock. Another important advantage is the ease of installation. For l-v lighting you need a transformer to reduce 120-volt household current to the 12-volt current required. Most modern garden-light transformers simply plug into any outlet. From the transformer on, the 12-volt wiring is buried a few inches in the ground, strung along fences or run up tree trunks — without the need of conduit or protected cable, as would be necessary with 120-volt wiring.

THE USE OF LOW-KEY LIGHTING

Low voltage garden lighting also allows you to have what is called low-key lighting. Low-key lighting is not only ample for illumination but is extremely flattering to a garden patio or entryway in its visual effects. It lets you create soft shadows and silhouettes with plants and accent architectural features—quite the opposite from what is achieved with floodlights. With such floodlighting an entry or garden is strongly illuminated for a short distance away but the light is flat and monotonous.

Creating low-key effects is a matter of experimenting with light in different places and different ways in your garden. With l-v equipment, you can simply string the wiring on top of the ground, and leave it there for weeks, if necessary, until you decide exactly where each fixture should be placed.

SOME BASIC RULES

Each garden is different, but here are some factors that lighting experts keep in mind on almost all l-v installations:

1. Try to use six or more small lights throughout your garden, rather than two or three more powerful lights.

2. Place lights out beyond your patio. There, they create depth in the garden, and they draw insects away from the patio.

3. Install separate switches for bright "activity" lights, such as near a barbecue or table tennis area, so they can be turned off when not needed.

4. Consider using a few small lights on a fence or hedge, if needed, as a curtain between your garden and a neighbor's.

5. Light the hazards (softly) as well as the attractive features. You know where a garden step is, but guests may not.

6. Use submersible fixtures in wet areas and garden pools, or else waterproof the connections thoroughly with a rubber seam compound. You can place any l-v fixture in water, but exposed connections will corrode and fail in time.

INSTALLATION IS IN TWO PARTS

Installation of l-v wiring is done in two steps. First, you connect a 12-volt garden transformer to a 120-volt outlet. Second, you run the low-voltage wiring out from the transformer to low-voltage light fixtures you have bought or made.

It's best to choose a transformer of about 100-watt capacity for your garden and patio — so you can run several lights (depending on size) from it. If you have a large lot, you may want to have a second garden transformer on the front side of the house, perhaps smaller for two or three lights. Avoid using doorbell transformers; most of them are unsafe for this use.

Try to install each transformer at some central location, so

Large entry fixture contains small bulb for soft light. Low-key 12-volt lights in the planter beds make pathway quite visible.

Perforated tubes are one of many low-voltage fixtures available; seem to twinkle as you walk past, cast shadows on tree fern.

two or more short cords can run from it to your lights, rather than one lengthy cord (there is more line-loss of current at 12 volts than at 120 volts). With the two-wire No. 12 cord generally used on low-voltage garden lighting, a run should not exceed 100 feet. If it needs to be longer, use heavier cord.

Installing the transformer. This can be done in several ways. The simplest is to obtain a transformer with a weatherproof case and plug-in cord, and just plug to an outlet on the patio, house exterior, or in the garage—as if it were a lamp.

If the outlet you choose is not controlled by a switch inside the house, you can use a transformer with a built-in switch. But this means that you will have to step outdoors to turn the lights on and off at the transformer, so it is usually better to rewire that outlet for a switch indoors. *If you are not familiar with house wiring, have an electrician do this job.*

Still another approach is to use automatic switching. You can buy l-v garden-light transformers today with built-in timers that automatically turn the garden lights on and off at any desired hours each evening. Or you can include a photo-electric switch at the outlet that will turn the lights on at sundown and off at dawn. With either, the efficient l-v lights use so little current that the expense of their being on for some extra hours is negligible.

Installing the wiring. The 12-volt cables running from the transformer to your garden lights are usually a "zipcord" type, similar in appearance to the cord for an electric toaster, only slightly heavier (two #12 wires) and with more weatherproof insulation.

You can bury these cords in the ground (in fact, it's best, as they then are protected from the sun). Place them 6 inches deep where possible, and try to run them alongside walks, fences, planter-bed edgings, and water lines, so you will not dig them up when cultivating.

Where a cord needs to cross a lawn, cut a slit-type trench, wedging it open with your shovel. Push the wire down into it and then tamp the turf back in place.

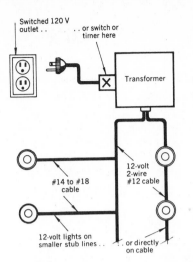

As shown in the drawing above, you can connect your garden lights along the main cords (some fixtures simply snap on), or you can run stub lines to different fixtures. The latter is preferable when you wish to install a fixture upon a fence or above an entryway, because you do not need to run the stub line farther to other lights, and it can be a small cord, even the #18 zipcord used on table lamps. You can hide this cord quite easily along wood and masonry joints, and along moldings.

For a fixture in a tree, just staple a cord up the back side of the trunk. Attach it loosely to allow for the tree's growth.

You can connect a stub line to a main cord with soldered joints, or screw-on or crimp-on connectors. With the latter two, coat the finished connections with any rubber seam compound —not for shock protection, but to prevent fertilizers and the like from corroding the connections.

When you stake a light fixture in the ground (rather than attaching it to a wall or other structure), bury at least a foot of slack cord alongside it to provide for future adjustments of the fixture as the plantings around it grow.

Hazardous steps are lighted by clay Mexican bell under railing. The bell's clapper is replaced by a small low-voltage light bulb.

Hanging planters act as light fixtures, contain cool 12-volt electric lights that are not harmful to the asparagus ferns.

Garden pools

Most people are attracted to water by its sight and sound. A garden pool can satisfy the desire to be near water, or to see it, or even play in it one way or another.

There are types of pools to satisfy almost every taste. A shallow reflecting pool may be all you need. Or, you may want a pool as big as the floor of your living room. The photographs on these two pages illustrate that there is no set design pattern for a garden pool. (The following five pages show still further examples of building garden pools — from a pool large enough for wading to a pool that is light enough to be portable.) The two pools shown below are built of bricks; the three on the opposite page are built of poured concrete.

USING BRICKS OR CONCRETE BLOCKS

The first step is to prepare the concrete floor. Once poured, the floor needs only two days to set up before the brick walls can be laid — but walk lightly on the floor. Below-grade brick walls are made of double rows of bricks laid end to end to make a wall 8 inches thick. Bricks for the top course are laid side by side. The mortar joints should be ½ inch thick and the finished walls should be coated with a waterproofing compound.

USING CONCRETE IN FORMS

The three concrete pools shown on the opposite page use a standard formula for the concrete: 1 part cement, 2 parts sand, and 3 parts gravel. The top and center pools are made in two pours. The first pour provides a 4 to 6-inch thick floor. The wall forms are staked in place on the floor and the second pour brings the pool walls to their final height. The lower photo shows a below-grade concrete pool that is built without a regular form. A 4-inch-wide trench is dug first and lined with asphalt paper, then filled with concrete. The concrete floor is poured last.

A TWO-SECTION GARDEN POOL

This richly planted pool has separate sections for bog plants and for water plants. A brick wall divides the bog section from the main body of the pool which contains water 18 inches deep. Walls are double rows of bricks with vertical reinforcement, and are waterproofed.
Design: Osmundson-Staley.

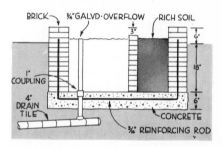

POOL FOR A GARDEN CORNER

Pie-shaped pool is set near a walk leading to the house. Straight sides of the pool are 6 feet long; curved edge is self-reinforcing. A drain in the bottom makes it easy to change water and clean the pool. Water lilies and hyacinths grow in pine planter boxes set on pool floor.
Design: Osmundson-Staley.

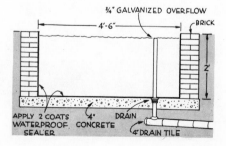

POOL IS FOCAL POINT OF GARDEN

This 6 by 10-foot pool is not difficult to build and provides ample space for fish or plants. The walls are 6 inches thick, are reinforced with wire mesh, and have a smooth finish. When the concrete has partially set up, fill the pool with water to help speed up the curing time.

Design: Portland Cement Association.

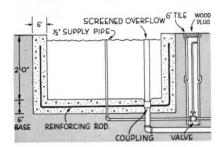

A REFLECTING OR WADING POOL

The outside form for this shallow pool rests on the ground; the center form hangs from ears from top edge of outer form — its depth is 4 inches shallower. Make your first concrete pour level with bottom of inside form. Let concrete set; make second pour up to top of all forms.

Design: Osmundson-Staley.

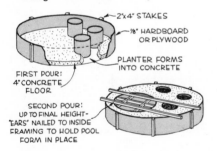

POOL WITH GRACEFUL CURVES

The graceful design of this pool was achieved by pouring concrete into a curved trench that had been lined with asphalt paper on the inside edge. The concrete was allowed to set up for one week before the interior of the pool was excavated and the concrete floor poured.

Design: L. Raymond Hodges.

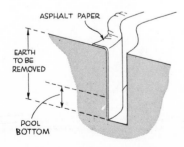

Garden pool with a fountain

Pool with fountain *is 2 feet deep, excellent for fish and water plants. Its walls are extra wide to serve as garden benches.*

Ordinarily, you would need to drain and scrub a pool of this type about twice a week to keep it clear of dirt and algae. But, though it contains fish and plants, this pool needs cleaning only about three times a year. One reason is that it contains a 21 by 31-inch plastic filter that is connected to a small, submersible pump. The pump draws the water down through a 2-inch bed of aquarium gravel and through the filter. The filter is really just a large flat screen; dirt and algae are trapped in the fine gravel above it and are consumed there by bacteria. The clear water is discharged through the fountain outlet and by-pass valve.

The pool's design is another reason for its low maintenance. It has a row of 4-inch Mexican ceramic tile at the water line for easy sponge-cleaning of the dust ring. Raised benchlike sides form barriers to keep out leaves and dust, windblown across the patio floor. Smooth vertical walls and rounded corners discourage algae, and the graveled bottom forms a neutral background so that whatever settles to the bottom isn't conspicuous.

The plumbing is unusually simple. If anything clogs the pump or filter, you can just lift out the entire system to clean it. The small head on the fountain (see drawing below) gives a gentle musical spray and the submerged pump makes no noise.

This pool needs no drainage system. You simply screw a ½-inch pipe-hose fitting to the fountain head and use the pump to empty the pool, running the water through a hose to nearby planting beds. In addition, there is no unsightly overflow fixture. The copper conduit for the pump's cord and another for a low-voltage underwater light will drain off any excess rainwater.

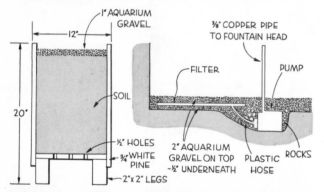

Planter box *has short legs, so that the fish can swim and hide underneath. Gravel covers filter, pump, entire bottom of pool.*

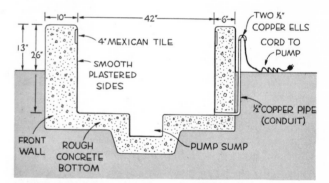

Cross-section *of pool shows that only the piping cast in concrete is copper conduit, which also serves as an overflow pipe.*

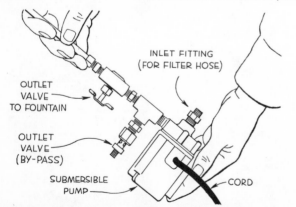

Compact pump *is fitted with two valves to adjust the fountain's flow, yet retain full flow of water through the gravel filter.*

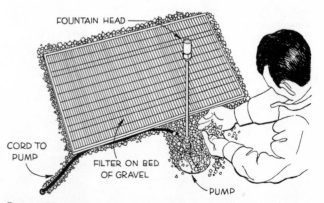

Removable pump *is secured and covered in small sump with gravel. Pump cord leads off to conduit in pool wall at the left.*

A pool for dunking or wading

Using the simplest construction methods, you can build a dunking pool like the one shown at right in a few weekends. Begin by outlining the shape you want on compact and unfilled ground. Then remove dirt inside this outline sloping the banks from the top and digging down about 4½ feet at the bottom. Build temporary forms around the top edge of the excavation using strips of quarter-inch plywood about six inches wide. Level these forms by placing a straightedge across the pool and checking with a level. Next, place wire mesh over the dug-out area, blocking it up about two inches from the earth with small pieces of brick (see sketch below).

Use a very dry concrete mix for the pool floor—1 part cement to 2½ parts sand, 3½ parts gravel—and very little water. Don't expect this mix to pour; a handful of it dropped on the ground should stand in a blob. Hand pack the concrete on the walls of the pool, starting from the bottom up. Leave a hole for the sump at the low point of the pool and set in a chrome-plated drain. Keep the concrete about four to five inches thick over the entire area. Trowel the surface with a curved steel trowel, bent to the minimum inside radius of the pool. Cure by sprinkling at hourly intervals during the first day after pouring, and about five or six times daily for about a week. While the concrete is setting up, you can remove the forms around the edge at the top and set in the brick coping.

Architect: B. F. Lippold.

Kidney-shaped pool is 18 feet long, 9 feet wide; was built entirely on original, unfilled ground dampened for easy digging. Site should be sheltered location that is almost level.

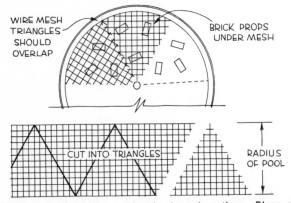

Wire mesh should be cut in pie-shaped sections. Place each section so that it will overlap the next section by at least 1 foot.

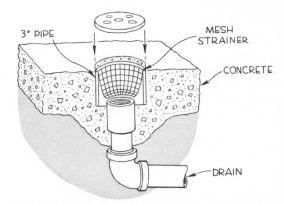

Gravity drain works just like a bathtub; requires that some point of surrounding area be lower than bottom of pool or pump.

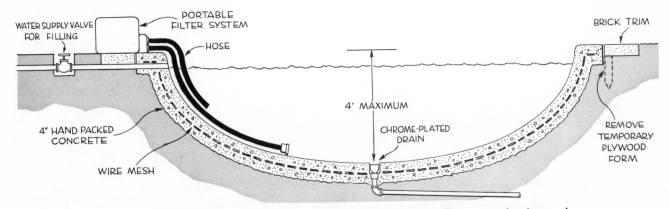

Cross section of pool shows gravity drain set 4 feet below the water surface. Portable filter system has hoses of different lengths for circulating the pool water. Forms at edges can be removed after the concrete sets up slightly.

AN EASY WAY TO POUR A GARDEN POOL

One of the easiest ways to construct a small pool is shown in the sketches here.

The ground underneath should be well packed to form a base for the concrete. Keep the trenches for pipes as small as possible and refill with gravel. Provide a cushion of tamped sand; if you live in a climate where the soil freezes and heaves in winter, or if the soil is adobe, use 3 or 4 inches of tamped sand and gravel. For the concrete, use a fairly dry and stiff mixture of about 1 part cement, 2 parts sand, and 3 parts gravel.

Design: Lawrence Halprin.

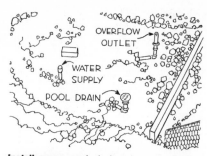

Install pump and drain pipes in narrow trenches at bottom of excavation for pool. Spread cushion of sand, gravel over area.

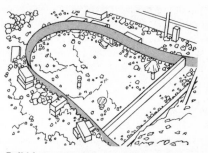

Build forms of wood or metal around top of pool to give finished edge. Drain grate marks the level of the finished pool floor.

Pour stiff concrete into depression and trowel smooth with a wood float. Wire mesh gives added strength to pool floor.

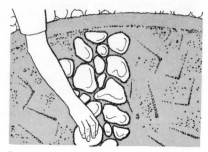

Press rocks or pebbles into concrete before it starts to set up, for a decorative effect. For a smooth finish, use a steel trowel.

Completed pool has medium-sized recirculating pump installed behind stone wall to give a gurgling sound effect of water.

HOW TO BUILD A POOL FOR FISH

Building a hillside garden pool large enough for fish may require several weekends of work. Although this pool was constructed on a slope of ground where a drainage ditch could carry off dirtied and muddied water, you could also install a drain or filter system (see pages 80 and 81).

On a slope, begin by removing soil to get a deep enough basin for the pool to be anchored. On the downhill slope construct a retaining wall of backfill and rubble concrete. Drive stakes into the ground to establish a level for pouring the concrete.

Design: William Steward.

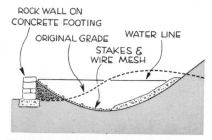

Excavation was held to minimum on hillside setting. Rock wall across one side rests on concrete footing; acts as dam.

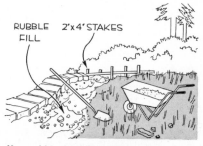

Use rubble backfill against stone wall to provide gradual slope to pool bottom. Deepest point of pool is 2 feet.

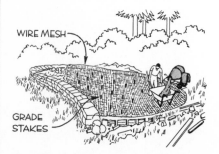

Use stakes in grid pattern to guide depth of concrete floor. Cover bottom of pool with chicken wire for reinforcing.

Trowel concrete into place with wood float. Use fine spray to keep concrete damp for 3 days, then fill pool with water.

Free-form concrete pool has drainage and overflow gravel ditch built around three sides to carry away runoff from winter rains.

Falling water in the garden

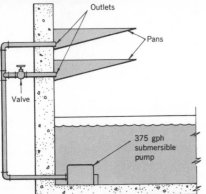

Water overflows from copper pans. Submerged pump delivers the water through simple piping. Design: Osmundson & Staley.

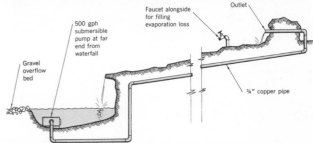

Trickling stream is recirculated, carried 8 feet up and 60 feet away by pump located in bottom of pool. Design: Michael Wills.

Cascading water over the steps of volcanic rock set in mortar gives off a pleasant musical sound (the water volume is considerable). Design: Raymond Hodges.

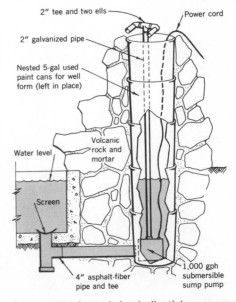

Large pump is sunk (and silent) in masonry well. The pipe and pump can be removed.

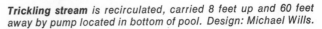

Indoor-outdoor pool

This simple fountain pool is pumped by a quiet, 1/55 hp submersible motor. The pump is bolted to the bottom of a shallow plastic pan, and has a short inlet that extends up through a hole cut in the pan. It draws water down and then returns it through a short hose.

To drain and clean such a pool, just tip the pan up to dump out the water. If the pool is indoors, slip a short length of hose over the fountain head and pump the water into a pail.

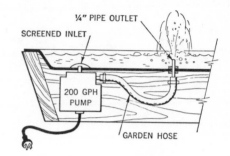

Fountain pool has submersible, noiseless pump; its plumbing is completely hidden. Just 3 feet square, the pool is portable.

Plumbing consists of a small pump near one corner of the pool. A short length of garden hose is attached to a central outlet.

Portable garden pool

This simple and portable pool can be constructed by using 2 by 12's for the sides and 2 by 10's for the top trim. Make all joints watertight by using a generous number of galvanized screws and then sealing with a rubber marine seam compound (available at boat supply stores). The pump is a small magnetic-drive submersible pump that delivers 170 gallons per hour. Its waterproof cord leads out of the pool through a small caulked hole at ground level. A garden hose (perforated every 2 inches with a 3/32-inch drill through both sides) on the bottom of the pool draws the water in for the fountain. The hose is plugged at the far end with a cork and is covered with a 2-inch layer of aquarium gravel. As the water is drawn through the fine gravel, algae are trapped in it and destroyed by bacteria, as in an aquarium.

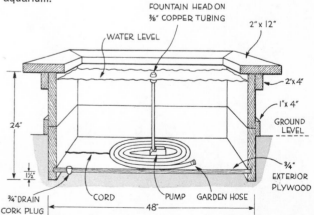

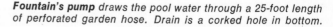

Top and sides of garden pool are redwood. Inside of pool is painted black with emulsified asphalt. Joints are water-tight.

Fountain's pump draws the pool water through a 25-foot length of perforated garden hose. Drain is a corked hole in bottom.

PUMP AND PLUMBING SYSTEMS FOR POOLS AND FOUNTAINS

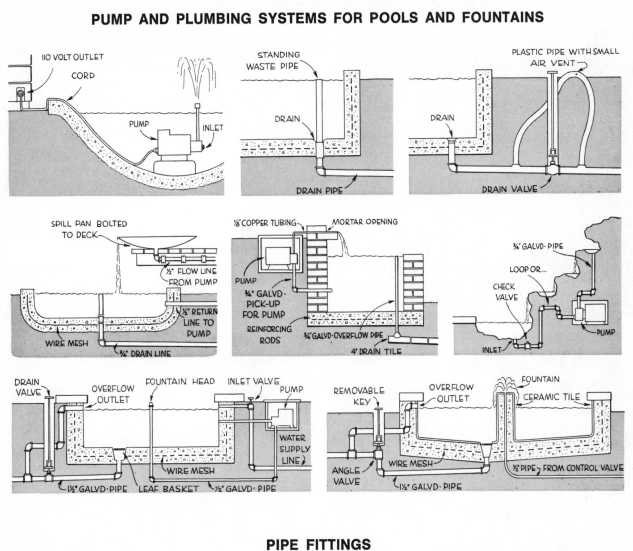

PIPE FITTINGS

Common pipe fittings are illustrated here as follows: (1) Coupling is common fitting to join two pipe sections of same size. (2) Tees allow pipe to tap into line (a reducing tee connects small pipe to large line. (3) Plug and cap are used to seal ends of lines. (4) Nipples are short, threaded lengths of pipe, usually used to connect up fixtures. (5) Bushing and reducer joins pipes and fittings of unequal sizes. (6) Unions connect two pipes where neither can be twisted to thread together with a coupling. (7) Elbows for changing direction of pipes.

More ideas for garden and patio building

Space is left between wire mesh fence and floor for easy cleaning with a hose.

Partial roof and the house give shelter, and the two rear fences give wind protection; the wire fencing permits a view. The run is 6 by 20 feet, ample for medium-sized dogs.

Corners of posts are covered with inexpensive corner metal to prevent chewing.

. . . how to plan a dog run

A dog run, just as the name implies, is an outdoor enclosure long enough to allow a dog to run. The run shown above can be modified to fit any size dog.

The floor of the run. The surface or floor of a dog run should provide a solid, rough footing. Concrete is generally regarded as the best surface, and, if possible, should be used for at least a part of the run, particularly in the sunning and feeding area. When laid, it should be rough-troweled or brushed, not "steeled" to a smooth, slippery finish.

Another answer is to build a simple 3 to 4-foot-square wooden platform on four 2 by 4 legs. Your dog can jump up on it to look around, and can rest beneath it in the shade.

Asphalt is a poor surface for a dog run, because it is absorbent and gets hot and often tacky on a warm day.

Gravel is good. It provides good drainage, changes temperature slowly, and provides the best possible footing for a dog. Because it is somewhat difficult to clean, gravel in a run should be removed and replaced about once a year. For a good gravel run, lay a foundation of about 8 inches of crushed rock, then cover with 2½ to 3 inches of pea gravel.

The fencing. The fencing can be of almost any material. Wire is usually least expensive, and it gives your dog a chance to see what is going on around him. Wood or other solid paneling gives good wind protection and some degree of shade. A combination of wire and solid fencing as used in the run shown here is excellent.

Height of the fencing depends more on the type of dog than his size; some small dogs are "jumpers," whereas larger but short-legged breeds such as the dachshund and Welsh corgi seldom jump. About 3 to 4 feet is a safe height for toy breeds. Collies require 5 feet, Airedales 7 feet, German shepherds 8 feet.

If you use welded wire for the fencing, 12½-gauge galvanized is satisfactory (and inexpensive) for all breeds of dogs. Chain-link wire fencing costs slightly more. Quite a few twisted wire fencings are also suitable. For small dogs, a twisted wire fencing of 16 to 18 gauge with 1-inch mesh is satisfactory; for large dogs, 12-gauge with 3-inch mesh is good.

String the wire on either steel or wooden posts, placed not more than 8 feet apart. You can use steel T-posts for wire fencing, but round pipe posts are preferable at the gate. Particularly at the gate, set fence posts at least 2 feet deep in concrete.

Welded wire needs no reinforcing, but chain-link and most twisted wire fencings are limber. They should be strengthened with a horizontal pipe along the top or with taut reinforcing wires at top, bottom, and center. Otherwise a dog can jump on the wire and bend it enough to climb it.

. . . a concrete bird bath

This concrete bird bath is as spacious as a good sized puddle and shallow enough to make a pleasant splashing place for birds of all sizes; it also fills itself. To make one like it, follow these step-by-step directions:

Making the base. Dig a hole about a foot deep and 20 inches square at the spot where you want to build the bird bath. Install a pipe from the house water line to the bird bath as shown in the sketch below, using an elbow joint to bring it up perpendicular to the base.

Making the pedestal. Make a form of 30-inch lengths of 1 by 8-inch lumber around the water pipe and over the hole, supporting it with two 2 by 4's (see sketch below). Drill a hole about 2 inches from the top on one side of the form to bring the end of the water pipe through. Nail ¾ by 1½-inch stock in the inside corners of the form to reinforce it and at the same time give a design to the pedestal. Pour in the concrete. (It takes about two wheelbarrow loads.)

Before the concrete sets, push two 30-inch-long reinforcing rods down into it. Also, place a metal flange—12 inches in diameter—on top, holding it in place near the center by running two galvanized bolts through the metal into the wet concrete.

After the concrete has seasoned for 15 days, remove the forms and fasten the flange securely in place by tightening nuts onto the bolts.

Making the platform. Take two pieces of ⅜-inch plywood, each 4 feet long and 2 feet wide. Cut a half circle in each piece so the plywood can be fitted around the flange and be flush with its surface. Nail the two pieces of plywood together so they can be easily knocked off later. Nail a leg to each corner of the plywood platform to hold it in place.

For sides of the form, use 2 by 4's, 38 inches long. Fit them together so the end of one board butts the side of the next. Be sure they are straight and level. Within the square formed by the 2 by 4's, fit a square of 1½ by 2½-inch lumber as shown in the sketch. This will form the lip around the edge of the platform. Place a wooden dowel at one spot along this lip to make a hole for the water line (see detail in the sketch below).

Lay four ⅜-inch reinforcing bars in a grid pattern on the bottom of the form before pouring the concrete. Use a piece of 1½ by 2-foot stock nailed to a 4-foot board to float the concrete and shape the bowl. Dust cement lightly over the top and hand trowel the surface to make it smooth. When the concrete has hardened, remove all forms.

Use copper tubing to connect the water line with a float valve (the type sold for watering poultry) at one side of the platform.

Making a portable bird bath. First, form a mound of moist earth not more than 3 inches high upon a flat surface such as plywood or hardboard. The mound may be shaped unevenly by hand or more exactly with a template made from a board curved to form the inner surface of the shallow pool. The interior texture of the finished bath depends on the smoothness of the dirt mound before the mix is poured. Don't make the surface too smooth; birds don't like a slick surface.

Around the finished mound, build a wooden frame of 1 by 6-inch lumber in the dimensions you want the finished pool to

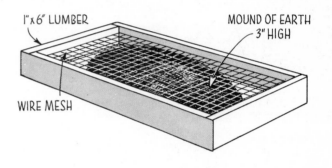

1"x6" LUMBER — MOUND OF EARTH 3" HIGH — WIRE MESH

be. The depth of this form must be 1 to 2 inches higher than the earth mound (see sketch above). Grease it well with light engine oil.

Pour just enough concrete mix into the form to settle around and over the earth mound. Lay a piece of wire mesh over the mound to strengthen the floor of the bird bath. Fill the frame to the top with concrete.

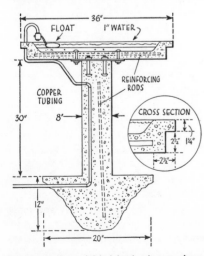

Cross section of bird bath shows placement of water pipe and reinforcing rods.

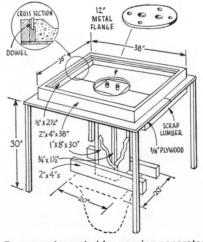

Framework needed for pouring concrete; mix of 1 part cement, 4 parts rock, sand.

Bird bath is large enough for bathing and drinking; is connected to water line.

. . . pivoting fence panels

One way you can provide privacy and control breezes without completely cutting off the view is to use flat panels of fiberglass in movable louvered frames. Each frame pivots on an ordinary nail and friction holds it in place. Drill a hole through the top and bottom rails for each frame slightly larger than the nail. Put the screen in place and hammer a nail through the holes into each screen frame. For a smoother finish, you can cut the head from a 10-penny nail and countersink it (see sketch below).

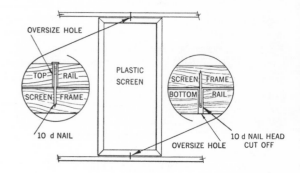

Movable louvers of white fiberglass, each 18 by 60 inches, are framed in 2 by 3-inch fir strips having mitered corners.

Screens pivot on a single nail driven through the outer structure into top and bottom of each panel. Louvers operate separately.

. . . simple screens for daytime privacy

Perhaps a screen outside a window may give you the privacy you desire when neighbors or front sidewalks are uncomfortably close to a living area.

For the screen pictured below on the right, simple vertical slat panels of 1 by 2's are set on edge and held together by ¾-inch dowels inserted through holes drilled in the slats. The panels are supported on two wood strips nailed horizontally to the window frame. They're secured to the house with gate hooks and are easily removed for window washing.

The screen on the left below was made of 2 by 4's spaced with short 4 by 6-inch blocks.

Baffle is anchored to concrete wall that runs below the living room window; provides privacy from the nearby street traffic.

Panels of 1 by 2's, on edge, screen tall and narrow windows; are lightweight and can easily be removed for window cleaning.

... storage cabinet for barbecue equipment

For those who do a great deal of outdoor cooking in the summer, an outdoor barbecue cabinet like the one shown here keeps all the necessary equipment close at hand and ready to use. It's attached to the wall of the house adjacent to the patio.

The cabinet is made of redwood to match the house siding and is stained the same color, so when it's closed it blends with the wall.

The same cabinet idea could be used on a garden screen or attached to the wall of a dressing room near a swimming pool. If you set it up some distance from the house, it might be a good idea to enlarge the cabinet to include storage for dishes, flatware, glasses, and one or two sturdy trays.

Bi-folding doors *close the upper portion of cabinet. Top is flat, has a 2-inch overhang; overall size is 44 by 27 by 12 inches.*

Drop-down counter *(11 inches deep) provides work counter space and place for hibachi, has chain support on each end.*

... a place to hide the garbage can

This cover-up box on a concrete pad next to the garage wall provides quick access to the garbage can and gas meter. The top slopes gently and overhangs 2 inches for rain run-off.

The box frame of 2 by 4's was attached to two front corner posts (4 by 4's sunk in concrete) and covered with sheets of ⅝-inch exterior plywood overlaid with 1 by 4's spaced about one inch apart. The unit measures 57 inches long, 24 inches wide, 36 inches high at the front, and 39 inches at the back. Its door has two 6-inch T-hinges and fastens with a cabinet catch. The wood is finished with water seal over shingle stain.

Cabinet lid *is two feet square, lifts up for garbage deposit. The 1-inch vent holes on the ends are screened on the inside.*

Door swings open *for garbage collecting and meter reading. Diagonal 2 by 3 braces top, which can be used as work surface.*

. . . a planter box to hide a handrail

This combination handrail and planter separates a streetside carport from a stairway leading down to an entry. Trailing lobelia interspersed with campanula grows in the planter, spilling over the sides to soften the hard line of the rail. Water simply drains through the cracks between the redwood pieces.

A supporting 4 by 4-inch post holds ends of upper and lower pairs of 2 by 4's between which run vertical 2 by 4's on edge (see sketch below). Handrail is 36 inches from the carport floor.
Architect: Lawrence Steiner.

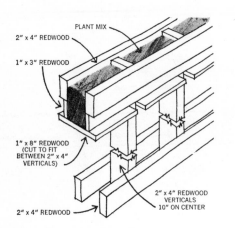

Detail sketch of handrail shows structure, primarily redwood 2 by 4's, with the plant mix supported by 1 by 3's and 1 by 8's.

Cascading lobelia provides pleasing effect to functional handrail. Soil drainage is through cracks in redwood planter box.

. . . how to plant beside a pool

You can avoid a harsh, barren effect around your swimming pool by eliminating the decking along one side of the pool and planting almost to the water's edge. This gives the pool a much more natural appearance and lets it blend with the rest of the landscape. A masonry wall separates the planting area from the pool; planting is out of range of splashing water.

In most cases it isn't difficult to add this kind of planting bed to your present pool. You should consult a pool contractor or landscape architect, however, before removing the coping and decking. (Most city or county building departments require a 4-foot-wide, solidly paved deck around pools that are built in expansive clay soil.)

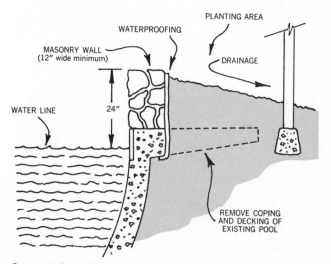

Masonry wall next to the pool has planting behind it to add beauty; eliminates unneeded decking along one side of pool.

Cross section of pool wall: After removing the coping and deck, add masonry wall that is 12 inches wide and 24 inches high.

. . . curbs and mowing strips

A curbing-mowing strip combination-separating a flower bed from a lawn area can cut down on the time needed for the trimming and edging necessary to keep a garden neat. Even a mowing strip alone has advantages. It contains the lawn in a fixed area, and it helps prevent excessive water run-off because it forms a low dam around the lawn. If the strip is a foot or more wide, you can use it as a path so you don't have to walk on wet grass or push a heavy wheelbarrow over the lawn.

Here is one way to install a curbing-mowing strip combination using such materials as marble, concrete blocks, or brick for the curb, and concrete for the strip.

Soak the ground the night before you begin work. Drive 3 by 72-inch lengths of 18-gauge galvanized metal or redwood into the ground following the curvature desired. The tops of these forms should be level with the soil. Dig a trench 2½ inches deep and 4½ inches wide, plus the thickness of the curbing material selected, behind the forms.

For the mowing strip, use a mix containing 2 parts rock and 3 parts sand to 1 part cement. Pour 1 inch of this mix in the bottom of the trench. When the concrete is firm, but not hard, set the curb in place. A little soil piled behind will help support cracks in the concrete, lay a ¼-inch reinforcing rod (two if you have adobe soil) along the mowing strip on top of this first con-

crete layer; or use short pieces of wood at intervals along the strip for expansion joints. Extend the rods out from the ends in case you wish to add to the strip at a later date.

Then fill the trench to the top of the metal or wood form with more concrete. Tamp with a block to bring the cement to the surface. Trowel lightly and clean the curb with a wet rag. When the concrete begins to set, trowel it smooth. After three days, remove the metal or wood form.

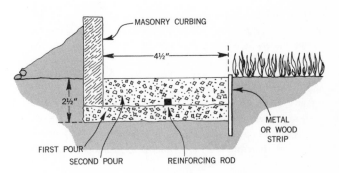

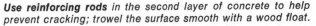

Use reinforcing rods in the second layer of concrete to help prevent cracking; trowel the surface smooth with a wood float.

. . . planting by a retaining wall

The L-shaped footing at the base of most masonry retaining walls will limit what you can plant there. You may not have the 6 to 12-inch-deep soil needed for lawn or annuals; and you're quite unlikely to have the 24 inches or more needed for most shrubs. Nevertheless, there are several choices of plant ma-

terial that will thrive in shallow soil. Also, there are several ways of building up a limited planting area at the base of a retaining wall.

If the soil is too shallow for the kind of planting you want, here are ways to solve the problem.

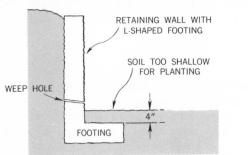

Shallow footing next to wall limits depth of soil for planting.

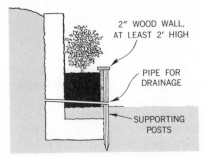

Build wood wall of 2-inch lumber to height of at least 2 feet.

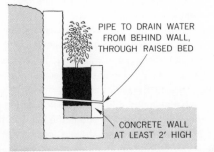

Add concrete wall at lower height to hold soil for raised bed.

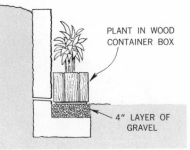

Set planter boxes or individual pots on 4-inch layer of gravel.

. . . how to make garden flats

Even an inexperienced carpenter can build flats or boxes for starting plants from seed or cuttings; and if you build your own, you can suit their shapes and sizes to your requirements.

Most nurseries sell flats but have them on hand only in the spring. Making your own is a worthwhile job if you need very many. Use cedar for its resistance to decay: either rough-cut boards or ¾-inch stock.

Use rust-resistant galvanized or aluminum nails. Be sure to leave ¼ inch of space between the bottom boards of each flat for drainage.

Flats you buy from nurseries vary in width from 11 to 15 inches, in length from 20 to 22 inches, and in depth from 2 to 3 inches. There is enough space in one of these flats for about a hundred cuttings of many kinds of shrubs and perennials, or for several packets of seeds. When the seedlings are large enough to transplant, each standard flat will hold five or six dozen plants until they are ready to set out.

Here are two variations of the standard nursery flat that you may want to copy or adapt for your own purpose:

The flat shown in the sketch below is 14 inches square and 9 inches deep. The added depth—6 inches of space after the necessary 3 inches of pure sand is laid in—protects summer cuttings of perennials, rock plants, and deciduous and evergreen shrubs from drying winds. In summer, a slatted wood cover is used for shade. The same cover can also be used to protect cuttings in very cold weather.

The 4 by 8-foot flat or propagating bench shown below stands 2 feet above the ground on two pipes and was designed especially for growing slow-germinating, hard-coated seeds of hardy shrubs, vines, and trees. If planted in smaller flats or in the ground, the seeds may be neglected, walked on by dogs, harvested by squirrels and bluejays, or nibbled by slugs just as they sprout. A cover lined with chicken wire helps keep birds and rodents away.

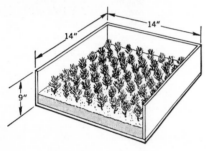

Deep flat gives hardy evergreen cuttings some protection from drying wind; use slatted cover for shade protection in summer.

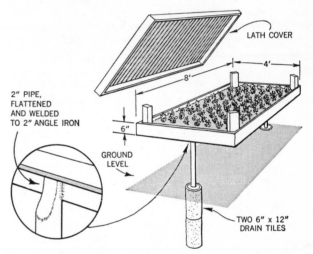

Giant flat is 4 by 8 feet; most useful for the slow-to-germinate shrub and tree seeds. Bricks at corners support the lath cover.

. . . a frame to support plants

Most annual bedding plants and many perennials that grow a foot or more in height require support.

The plant support described below works particularly well in beds bordering walks or adjacent to a fence.

To make this plant support, you'll need a 1 by 1-inch rail (length as needed); ¼-inch wooden dowels, about 1 foot long, to serve as dividers between individual plants; ⅜-inch dowels

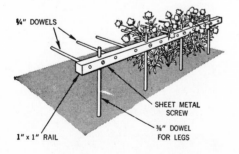

in 2-foot lengths, sharpened at one end, for legs; and ½-inch sheet metal screws for set screws.

Four legs provide good support for a 10-foot unit. Drill holes in the rail to accommodate these legs, large enough so the legs will slide easily in and out when wet. Drill a ⅛-inch hole in front of each leg hole for sheet metal screws. Loosen the screws to raise the rail as needed. Space ¼-inch dowels to correspond with the spacing of the plants in garden beds. Paint or seal all wood to prevent warping.

If the ends of the horizontal dowels rest against a wall or fence, the support is complete just as shown in the sketch. Otherwise, you may need a rear rail with legs like the front one.

If the weight of heavy foliaged plants tends to force the support forward, take two stakes about 15 inches long, sharpen one end of each stake, and drill a ¼-inch hole in the other end. Thread a strong piece of twine through the holes in the stakes. Push the stakes into the ground about a foot or so behind the ends of the support. Tie twine to the ends of the front rail.

Design: Harold Rawson.

. . . an easy-to-make soil sifter

To screen rocks and lumps out of the soil, sand, and leaf mold you use for seeding and potting mixes, you need a good garden sifter. A sifter is no trouble to make — just four 1 by 3 wood sides and a piece of galvanized hardware cloth (¼-inch mesh screen stapled across the bottom). But if you add an overlay of thin plywood or hardboard around the outside, you will improve it in these three ways:

The overlay gives a lip that holds the screen on your garden flats. It also covers the sharp edges of the wire screen. And

Stir soil or leaf mold with a trowel or a tool to sift it; or shake the sifter lightly being careful not to spill soil over the edges.

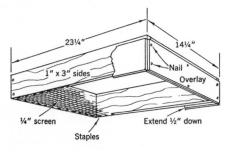

it keeps the nails in the corners of the 1 by 3 box itself from loosening after usage and weathering.

Make the 1 by 3 box just ¼ inch larger than the size of your garden flats. Tack the hardware cloth to the bottom, being generous with staples. Then nail the overlay of ¼-inch plywood, hardboard, or wood over the sides.

. . . how to build a rodent fence

If you garden in a rural area where visits by rabbits, squirrels, gophers, and moles are quite frequent, you may save yourself some work and grief by building a fence like this around your lot, your vegetable garden, or around your most valued plants. Here are the materials you would need to build a rodent-proof fence around a 30 by 30-foot plot:

—120 lineal feet of 1-inch mesh poultry screen, 48 inches wide. Get the best quality (galvanized after weaving).

—Twelve 2 by 4-inch posts, 48 inches long.

—Ten 2 by 3-inch underground post braces or lugs, 12 inches long.

—36 lineal feet of ¾ by 2-inch stock for gate pieces.

—12 building laths for gate slats.

—A 2 by 6-inch gate support, 36 inches long (it goes underground).

—1 pair T-hinges and 1 gate hook.

—Wood preservative, nails, and staples.

Paint or soak the bottom 16 inches of each post and the gate support with creosote, pentachlorophenol, or a copper compound wood preservative.

Lay out the fence's course and mark it with stakes and string. Drill holes for the fence posts and place them in the ground.

Dig a trench 6 inches deep and 8 inches wide along the outside face of the posts, all around the area.

Staple the wire mesh onto the posts, above and below grade level, as shown in the sketch.

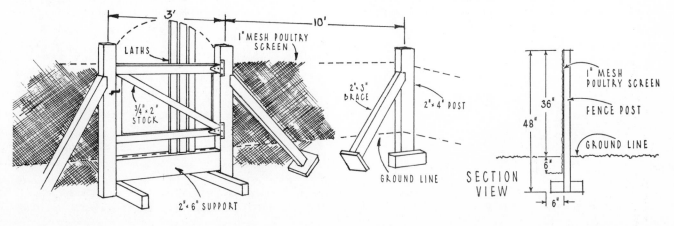

. . . a "floating" concrete terrace

Scalloped slab *is landing for stairway from upper level; provides pleasant place to sit. High screen protects against wind.*

An overhanging edge gives this concrete garden slab a floating appearance. It creates an intimate area for conversation, refreshments, or just sitting. The method for pouring such a slab is to mound up earth under the edge of the slab to be poured, then dig it away after the concrete has cured (see sketch below). The edge effects a graceful break with the ground.

First mound earth in a circle 6 inches high and 9 feet in diameter. Use two sticks and a rope as a compass to mark a circumference along the top of the mound. Then bend 6-inch-wide sheet metal to make a circular form for a slab 4 inches thick at the edge; stake it in place two inches down in the earth. (Corrugated sheet metal will produce a scalloped edge, but flat sheet metal works as well.) In the center, make another mound of earth to avoid filling with more concrete than necessary. Pour the concrete on standard reinforcing wire mesh.

Design: Lorrin Andrade.

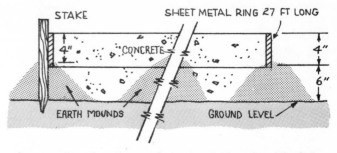

Cross-section *of earth mound, sheet metal form for slab. Outer earth ring is dug away; the inner mound is encased in concrete.*

. . . an easy-to-make garden bench

You can make this sturdy garden bench with just three saw-cuts: Cut a 50-inch length of rough 2 by 4 for the leg brace; cut two 13-inch lengths from an 8-foot plank, and you then have both legs and top.

Best width for the top is 14 to 16 inches. But you may find that some of the more commonly available 12-inch stock in your local yard is over 13 inches wide and wide enough.

The legs of the bench are secured to the 2 by 4 brace with two galvanized 20-penny common nails at each end and are toenailed to the top from below with 16-penny nails.

Design: George F. Malone.

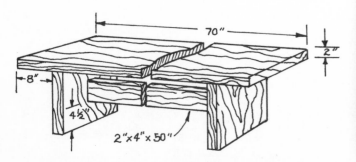

Brush waterproof glue *on all joints before assembling, or use ¼ by 5-inch galvanized lag screws and washers in drilled holes.*

Time required *to build this sturdy garden bench was 8 minutes. Bench requires no finish, and can be left to weather naturally.*

... nine special ideas for the garden

Hose guide is made with two 1 by 2-inch stakes and two 1 by 1-inch crosspieces; it is 14 inches tall and 8 inches wide.

Extension hose bib is made with two elbow joints, two lengths of pipe; screen fence projects out from the side of house.

Concrete basin poured between cardboard tubes catches rain run-off; has drain pipe. Architects: Kitchen and Hunt.

Pebble splash bed under the downspout breaks water fall, channels excess away from foundation to downslope at right.

Deep trench at the edge of driveway is filled with smooth gravel, collects and leads off surface water to a nearby drain.

Garden umbrella stand is made from a soy tub; vertical iron pipe holds the umbrella staff, is kept in position by rocks.

Bonsai stand is log section set on end with a concrete 12 by 12-inch stepping-stone. Design: Roy Rydell.

Wind Screen is a sheet of window glass set in a wooden frame cantilevered out beyond the sun deck and the house wall.

Screen for trash can is rough-cut 1 by 6's with 4 by 4-inch posts, and it is capped with 2 by 6's. Design: Chandler Fairbank.

Index

Photographers

Cover photograph by **Clyde Childress**. **William Aplin:** pages 27 (bottom right), 39 (bottom), 43 (top left). **Aplin-Dudley Studios:** page 75 (top). **Nancy Bannick:** page 26 (top right). **Ernest Braun:** pages 16 (top, bottom), 17 (center), 24 (top left), 36 (top), 43 (bottom left), 46 (bottom left), 47 (top left, top center), 83 (top left), 88 (bottom right). **Tom Burns, Jr.:** page 24 (bottom right). **California Redwood Association:** page 20 (bottom). **Clyde Childress:** pages 46 (bottom center, bottom right), 47 (center left, center), 95 (bottom center). **Glenn M. Christiansen:** pages 21, 23 (bottom), 47 (bottom right), 69 (top right), 93, 94 (bottom). **Thomas D. Church:** pages 47 (bottom left), 59 (middle center). **Robert C. Cleveland:** page 95 (center right). **Richard Dawson:** pages 22, 47 (center right), 95 (center left). **Dearborn-Massar:** pages 16 (center), 69 (bottom left), 95 (center). **Philip Fein:** page 59 (bottom left). **Richard Fish:** pages 17 (top), 24 (bottom left), 39 (top), 59 (top left), 69 (top left). **Roger Flanagan:** page 95 (top center). **Frank L.**

Gaynor: page 17 (bottom). **Art Hupy:** page 27 (top right). **Pirkle Jones:** page 23 (top). **George Knight:** page 95 (top right). **Roy Krell:** pages 38, 41 (bottom right), 59 (top center, top right, center right, bottom right), 67 (top right), 95 (bottom right). **Jack McDowell:** pages 46 (top right), 67 (bottom right). **Don Normark:** pages 41 (top left, center), 67 (bottom left). **Theodore Osmundson:** pages 36 (bottom), 47 (bottom center), 78, 79 (center). **Phil Palmer:** page 81. **Ray Piper:** page 94 (top). **Portland Cement Association:** page 79 (top). **Selwyn Pullan:** page 88 (top). **Tom Riley:** pages 79 (bottom), 83 (bottom), 84 (top). **John Robinson:** pages 43 (top right, center left, bottom right), 74 (top). **Martha Rosman:** pages 88 (bottom left), 89 (bottom), 90. **Julius Shulman:** page 59 (center left). **Douglas M. Simmonds:** page 75 (center). **Blair Stapp:** page 46 (top center). **Darrow M. Watt:** pages 20 (top), 24 (top left, bottom), 27 (top left, bottom left), 41 (top right), 43 (center right), 47 (top right), 67 (top left), 75 (bottom), 76, 77, 80, 83 (top right), 84 (bottom), 86, 89 (top), 95 (bottom left). **Ray O. Welch:** page 69 (bottom right). **R. Wenkam:** page 74 (bottom). **George Woo:** page 41 (bottom left).